The Boys from the Bridge

The story of
Attenborough's Private Army

The Boys from the Bridge

Sebastian Abineri

The Book Guild Ltd

First published in Great Britain in 2025 by
The Book Guild Ltd
9 Priory Business Park
Wistow Road, Kibworth
Leicestershire, LE8 0RX
Freephone: 0800 999 2982
www.bookguild.co.uk
Email: info@bookguild.co.uk
Twitter: @bookguild

Typeset in Minion Pro

Printed and bound in Great Britain by CPI Group (UK) Ltd, Croydon, CR0 4YY ISBN 978

ISBN 979-8-88771-771-5

British Library Cataloguing in Publication Data.
A catalogue record for this book is available from the British Library.

For Alexander…who taught me to love Rugby
and all my Old Mates in Attenborough's Private Army (APA)
wherever you may be!

Introduction by Dr David English CBE

During my seventy-year adventure on this planet, I am extremely fortunate to have formed or been part of some earth-shattering teams! I have played for Middlesex County Cricket Club at Lords and run the showbiz and entertainment category for the *London Evening News* and the *Daily Mail.* I was also Head of Press at Decca Records, looking after the Rolling Stones, the Moody Blues, Tom Jones and Engelbert.

Since forming RSO Records with Robert Stigwood, I have managed the Bee Gees and Eric Clapton and produced *Saturday Night Fever* and *Grease.* After a spell as an actor, I founded the Bunbury Cricket Club and raised £17Million for charity by playing fun-filled cricket matches for all the family through my Bunbury English Schools Cricket Festival.

I have discovered seventy-four England cricketers and 723 first class cricketers. It has been an honour and a privilege to be part of these teams.

Forty years ago I was fortunate to be part of an extra-special company of men in the making of the classic war film *A Bridge Too Far.* A lot of people still say to me, "Well, we watched *A Bridge Too Far* and we didn't see you in it... were you the third dead German from the left?"

It wasn't as simple as that; it was much, much more. It all started back in March 1976. Sir Richard Attenborough's film was based on Cornelius Ryan's book *A Bridge Too Far*, the tragic story of the Battle for Arnhem Bridge in Holland.

This, the greatest of all war films, featured some of the world's foremost stars, but the thing I remember best about it was the team. I joined fifty of the finest men I have ever met, blokes of all shapes, sizes and dispositions; a motley crew who were to be called Attenborough's Private Army. The APA was the Guvnor's brainchild.

He felt to complement his superstars he would need a band of young actors who, at any given time, could be asked to play a role or express a particular emotion.

A kind of repertory company who would be taught to live, think and act like soldiers.

For me the shining star of the APA… the man who epitomised the wonderful spirit and camaraderie of our magnificent fifty was Sebastian 'Seebo' Abineri.

I am proud and honoured to introduce you to his wonderful story of the APA *The Boys from The Bridge.*

For me, his words 'leap off the page' and paint memorable pictures of our time together in 1976

The hottest summer in Holland for 100 years!

Well played, Seebo… you would be number one on my team sheet… every time!!

"Where Lindsay Anderson calls me a really rude name!"

This story starts in 1975 on a Suffolk Farm: I'm up to my knees in silage and I'm busy forking it onto a trailer to feed the cattle. It's heavy, glutinous stuff; basically, it is chemically treated grass which weighs a ton.

Sweat's pouring off my twenty-year-old body and I smell atrocious.

Even though I'm quite enjoying working on this farm, it's not the way I saw my career going.

Three months earlier, I'd appeared in a leading role in a BBC play by Willy Russell called *The Death of A Young-Young-Man*. The part I played? An intellectually-challenged farm labourer – my big break!

I received good reviews, I asked all the casting directors and directors to watch it. 300 letters I wrote by hand, there being no computers then, letting people know it was on and three months later nothing… no phone calls from my agent… nothing.

I mused as I forked another load of stinking silage on to the trailer, "If this is a case of life imitating art then the fates are having a jolly good laugh."

I piled the last fork load of steaming silage on to the cart and leaned forward on my pitchfork to draw out my Old Holborn from my pocket to roll myself a cigarette before driving the tractor to the field to offload my cargo to the cattle in my care. It was nearly their lunchtime… and nearly mine, too.

The people I was working for on this farm were lovely, kind people who fed me well and tolerated my actor-ish 'townee' ways. When I started the job I didn't expect to last very long, as

I'd never done any form of hard labour before (I didn't really count carting scenery around as an assistant stage manager as hard labour). Yet these people didn't mind the fact that I had to cry off the hay-making halfway through my first day, as I was working in a ten-acre field in the blazing heat, miles from the house and had omitted to bring water. They also forgave me for falling asleep in the hay barn after lunch; I woke up at three in the afternoon one day with Bob working around me, stacking the hay bales.

"Why didn't you wake me?" I asked.

"You looked so peaceful lyin' there, booy, I didn't have the heart to disturb you!" Bob replied.

Even when Bob sent me once to fence off a twenty-acre field so that he could move his cattle to a fresh pasture, he just laughed when he appeared four hours later to witness me struggling in the middle of a huge bird's nest of tangled wire not having hammered in a single post.

"There's a knack to everythin', booy. Don't worry, you'll larn."

He was right, I did learn, and by the time I got to the stage of forking the silage I was a proficient son of the soil and actually beginning to enjoy my work. I was enjoying the fact that my body was beginning to turn into a sort of oak-coloured ditch-digging machine, that I could now get through the day without feeling exhausted, and also I was enjoying those wonderful Suffolk sunsets when walking home at nightfall.

A bell rang loudly outside the farmhouse: it was the telephone. I stuck my pitchfork into the heap of silage on the trailer and walked round to start the tractor.

Bob called from the front porch, "Sebastian, there's a phone call for you from London."

My Agent! I prayed, and trotted off towards the house.

Amazingly it *was* my agent. "Hi Bernard," I said.

"Sebastian I've just had Miriam Brickman on the phone and I have an appointment for you to meet Lindsay Anderson, he's starting a repertory company in the West End with Joan Plowright, Helen Mirren and Peter McEnery. They're going to be mounting *The Seagull* and a new play by Ben Travers called *The Bed Before Yesterday*. Even though Ben Travers is ninety, it's still a new play!"

"Fantastic," I replied.

Miriam Brickman was the top casting director at that time and had made the careers of many of our finest Actors, so it was vital that I made this casting.

"Can you make an appointment in Kennington for six o'clock this evening?"

"It's going to be tight," I said, "it's 12.30 now and I need to get home and have a bath, and then get myself down to Brampton station. I'll then need to change at Ipswich, but I'll do my best."

"Good," said Bernard. "I'll tell them you can make it." I put the phone down.

"Sorry, Bob, I've got to go," I said.

"That's orlright, booy… off you go and good luck."

I sprinted down the farm track in my wellington boots towards my house, which was about half a mile away. Five minutes later, I barrelled in through the front door, kicked my wellies off and headed upstairs for the shower, undressing as I went.

My mother said, "You're home early, darling."

"I know, Mum," I said. "I've just had a call from Bernard and I've got an audition with Lindsay Anderson for a new repertory company he's starting in the West End. I've got to be at Kennington at six o clock."

All this was being said as I headed for the shower.

I knew from bitter experience that, however hard I scrubbed, the smell of the silage would linger for at least three days. Nevertheless I scrubbed manfully and put my clean, smart clothes on and hared down the stairs where my mother was waiting for me in the Morris Traveller to take me to Brampton Station.

Brampton Station was one of those isolated, charming old Suffolk railway stations on the branch line from Ipswich to Lowestoft. A guard, rather like a bus conductor, used to walk up and down the train collecting payment for tickets from your station to Ipswich. When you arrived at Ipswich you had to buy another ticket to get down to London Liverpool Street.

Outside of the rush-hour the connections at Ipswich station for the London train were normally pretty ropey; very often you'd have to wait an hour or so before getting the London train, which is why going down to London and back for an audition used to take a whole day.

The guard on the Brampton train arrived to take payment for my ticket.

"Ipswich please" I said.

The guard sniffed the air around me, which was redolent with the odour of silage laced with Old Spice and Life-Boy Soap, then wrinkled his nose in distaste.

Blimey, I thought, you'd think he'd be used to the smell in this part of the world... mind you, most of the guys who smell like me live in remote parts of darkest Suffolk, and very rarely board trains to London to meet important theatre Directors like Lindsay Anderson. Oh Well!"

There was nothing I could do about my smell, or indeed the speed of the train, so I took advantage of the unexpected break from my labours on the farm and watched the familiar Suffolk countryside roll by me.

The train crawled in to Ipswich Station and I leapt out to buy myself a ticket for London. Sure enough, there wasn't another train to London for an hour.

I could feel the tension start to build as the clock crept towards 4:20pm, the time of the next train. At this rate I'd be at Liverpool Street by about 5.45pm, which would give me fifteen minutes to get to Kennington.

I went to a public phone box and phoned Bernard my agent to ask him to phone and tell them I'd been delayed and would they mind waiting fifteen minutes for me. Bernard took the number of the phone booth and five interminable minutes later he called me back to let me know that they'd wait; luckily, they were a bit behind anyway.

It was beginning to get dark as the train rolled in to Liverpool Street.

I ran from the train to the Underground and got to Kennington Oval at 6.20pm.

Fuck! I'm really late, I thought. It was a good ten minutes walk from the station to the Church Hall where they were holding the auditions.

I started to run, *A to Z* in one hand whilst my eyes cast around looking for the Church Hall. After running for about five minutes, I spied it in the gloom and sprinted through the door.

Thank God they were all still there chatting at the table.

I rushed up to them and proffered my sweaty palm to the man sitting in the middle who bore a passing resemblance to Julius Caesar. This, I assumed, was Lindsay Anderson.

By this time I was extremely hot, and sweat was rolling freely off my body. My attempts to mask the smell of silage with Old Spice & Life-Boy Soap had worn off long ago and the old church hall was filled with the pungent aroma of chemically-treated cattle feed, made worse by the heat of my body in the confined space.

"I'm terribly sorry I'm late," I gasped, "but the train—"
"What in the name of Christ is that bloody terrible smell?!"

Lindsay snapped.

"Erm… it's silage," I stammered.

"What's silage!" said Lindsay, squirming in his seat. "No, no… don't explain. Go and stand at the other end of the hall and tell me."

Absolutely mortified with embarrassment, which only served to raise my temperature even more thereby making the smell much worse, I trudged to the other end of the hall and turned round.

I took a deep breath and said, "Silage is chemically-treated cattle feed which I have been giving to the cows on the farm that I'm working on at the moment."

"You mean cows eat food that smells like that?" Lindsay said. "I'm going vegetarian then," said the man sitting beside him, who turned out to be Trevor Bentham, Lindsay's company

manager.

"The cows like it," I said lamely.

"I'm delighted for them," said Lindsay drily, regaining his composure somewhat.

"Now I'd like you to read a couple of scenes for me, if that's OK?"

"Fine," I said, and stepped towards them to pick up the script.

"Stay where you are!" roared Lindsay. "Don't you dare come any closer!"

Frisby-like, he skimmed the script across the room towards me.

I caught it. "Read the scene at the beginning of the play with Konstantin and Nina," he said.

I proceeded to read the scene with a girl reading Nina, who wisely stayed sitting beside Lindsay.

When I finished, I began to walk back to hand over the script.

"No! No!" said Lindsay. "Don't come any nearer, just throw it back."

I duly obeyed.

Lindsay looked towards Trevor Bentham, who nodded and Lindsay looked back to me.

"Well, we've decided to offer you a change from your bucolic labours and would like you to play a Russian Peasant in *The Seagull*, where you will combine the roles of understudy to Medviedenko and Assistant Stage Manager.

Delighted I moved towards Lindsay and Trevor to shake their hands.

Lindsay raised a hand. "Come any closer and I will withdraw this offer, and if you ever come to rehearsals smelling of silage – or whatever it is – you will be instantly dismissed…understood?"

"Understood!" I replied.

"Good," said Lindsay, a half smile playing across his lips. "See you at rehearsals then."

"Thank you!" I said, and left the room feeling like I was walking on air.

A few weeks later I bade my sad farewells to Bob at the farm and to my family. With a light heart and "a sense of destiny which hung about me like a spring cloud", I took the London train again to begin rehearsals.

I was going to be staying with my cousin who was a student at the Royal School of Music. I was given a room in a vicarage in Hampstead, with the run of the rest of the house, for the amazingly reasonable rent of £7 per week.

The only other stipulation being that I was to sing in the choir on Sundays, as they were short of a Baritone!

I was going to be earning the princely sum of £50 per week, plus overtime for production weekends, which at that time was a very generous stipend indeed.

Lindsay Anderson and H M Tennant were trying a new concept by attempting to run a repertory company in the West End. They were starting off by mounting Chekov's *The Seagull,* and once that was underway they would start rehearsals for a new play by the ninety-year-old Ben Travers, which was called the *Bed Before Yesterday* and followed the story of an older man who had lost his erection and was trying to find it again.

Lindsay had assembled a wonderful company, which included Helen Mirren; Joan Plowright; Peter McEnery; Frank Grimes; John Moffat; the lovely Patsy Rowland of *Carry On* fame; Leonard Fenton, who went on to play the doctor in EastEnders; Kevin Stoney; Neil Kennedy; and my humble self.

On the first day of rehearsals, we assembled at The Irish Club, in Belgravia of all places, and proceeded to read the play and get to know each other.

As I was an assistant stage manager and playing a small role I had plenty of time to observe the process.

I had done a lot of theatre since starting as an actor at the age of seventeen in weekly rep', which was basically, up until that time, my only experience of working in theatre, even though during that period I'd appeared in more than seventy productions.

Weekly rep', for the uninitiated, meant basically putting on a play every week. The company would rehearse one play during the day and perform another one in the evenings. At the end of the week, they would perform the play they had rehearsed during the days and then start rehearsing another one, this would sometimes go on for thirty weeks at a time.

This was wonderful experience, but didn't really give you much time to learn your lines let alone 'mine the text', so a five-week rehearsal period, which is what we had for *The Seagull* was a real eye-opener.

It gave, what was a very good company anyway, the time to discuss their characters and the opportunity to make choices as to how they would be played. That was the real value of a five-week rehearsal period. There are so many different ways that a good actor can approach a role, but being given the time to make the right choices under the guiding hand of a director like Lindsay Anderson brought a whole new dimension to everyone's work and was terrific experience for me, a young actor who was still learning his job.

It was fantastic watching Lindsay work. He was a highly intelligent man bordering on the intellectual really but with an accessibility which meant that you could almost tap into his intellect thereby temporarily enhancing your own. He was a director who loved actors and was loved by the actors in return. Unlike the other directors I'd worked with, who basically used to sit in the auditorium calling out to the actors from the stalls, Lindsay would be up on stage with you, scrutinising your performance from close range rather like he was directing a movie. Which of course he'd done anyway, directing films like *If*,

Oh Lucky Man, Britannia Hospital etc.

Things didn't always run smoothly, however: at one point in the rehearsals, Lindsay was trying to get something across to the company which they didn't really understand, and a lot of discussion was going on about how to resolve the problem. I thought I had the solution and was dying to make a suggestion but not quite daring to.

Lindsay noticed this and wheeled round saying to me. "Well, Sebastian, what do you think?"

I said, "It's alright, Lindsay, it doesn't matter."

"No, No," said Lindsay. "Never let it be said that this is not a democratic company where everybody can make their contributions… what's your suggestion?"

I put forward my idea, which as I remember basically consisted of re-staging the whole scene!

Lindsay stared at me for a long time.

"Nooo! You idiot!" he said, glaring at me like an outraged eagle… "You've completely missed the point! You know if you weren't so amiable Sebastian, you'd be a C**t!"

I staggered back in shock, horror and amazement!

The wonderful Joan Plowright, her protective instincts coming to the fore, rushed over to me and said, "Don't worry, darling, he's not angry with you its us stupid actors he's annoyed with… he just daren't call us that awful name!" She said, throwing an accusing look in Lindsay's direction.

*He called me a C**t*, I thought, *Lindsay Anderson called me a C**t!*

From that point on I was in thrall to him and gave him my undying loyalty and devotion… and to Joan Plowright, too.

After a few weeks rehearsing at the Irish Club we finally moved in to the Lyric theatre for the last two weeks before opening. It was good to get into the theatre and start familiarising ourselves with the surroundings that were going to be our home for the next nine months.

I was busy rehearsing my small role in *The Seagull*, making tea for the actors, going out and getting props, fetching Lindsay's lunch, indeed tackling any job that needed doing.

Lindsay called me over one day and said, "Sebastian, I need you to mock up a box of chocolates for Joan to dip into in Act 1. The box needs to have the name of a pre-revolutionary confectionery firm on the lid of the box and needs to be written in Cyrillic Russian."

I said, "Well, I can make the box, Lindsay, but I don't know the name of a Russian confectionery firm and I don't know how to write Cyrillic Russian."

Nowadays this would not be so much of a problem of course, as all of this research can be done over the internet. In those days, however, it would have meant a day's work trawling around the National Library and the British Museum.

"Don't worry about that," Lindsay said. "Here is a telephone number for Baronness Gallina von Meck, who is the Russian advisor to English theatre, give her a ring and she'll be able to help."

At lunchtime, I popped out to get Lindsay's customary midday meal of a chopped liver and gherkin sandwich on rye bread with a half bottle of red wine and on my way back I went in to the call box opposite the stage door and phoned Gallina Von Meck.

A cultured voice with a slight accent answered the phone. "Oh, hello," I said. "I've been given your name by Lindsay

Anderson, who said you might be able to help me."

"Oh Lindsay," she said. "How is he? Do give him my regards." "I certainly will," I said. "The thing is, we're in the middle of rehearsals for *The Seagull* at the moment and Lindsay has asked me to makeup a box of chocolates for Joan Plowright to use as a prop. I was wondering if you could possibly write down, in Cyrillic Russian, the word 'chocolates' and also the name of a pre-revolutionary Russian confectionary firm that I can then

copy on to the box."

"Of course I can, I'll do that now. Who shall I send it to?"

I said, "Can you send it to me, please? My name's Sebastian Abineri and if you could send it to care of the Lyric theatre, Stage Door, Gt Windmill Stree—"

She stopped me. "What did you say your second name was?"

"Abineri" I said, I was used to this. "You spell it A-B-I-N-E-R-I."

"Abineri?" she said.

"That's right," I said.

"How extraordinary," she said. "At the end of the war I was

in Germany helping to rehabilitate concentration camp inmates and I nursed two Abineri girls back to health; they then became my assistants and helped me nurse others. One of them married an Australian soldier and went to live in Australia and the other one married an American officer and they now live in the USA."

I fell silent. My Grandfather was born to a Jewish background from Vienna and had settled in England in 1911. In 1936, seeing the way things were going in Europe, he'd sent his son, my uncle Keith, across to Austria, Germany and Hungary to get as many of the family out as possible.

No one came with him except my grandfather's mother. None of the rest of the family believed anything was going to happen to them and we lost them all.

My grandfather believed that they'd all died in the Holocaust. Now, however, we'd found two girls, who we wouldn't have been able to trace even if we'd wanted to as of course they'd changed their names to their husbands'.

I told Gallina this and she said that she'd put the contact details for my relatives into the letter that she'd send me regarding the chocolates.

I walked slowly back to rehearsals pondering serendipity, kismet and the fates.

I duly passed this information on to my family and we became reunited with the two girls we thought we'd lost.

Looking back over the past thirty-odd years, I've come to believe there might have been something of the mystic about Lindsay. I remember reading much later about how he'd had an awful presentiment about the twin towers whilst flying round them in a helicopter.

He also predicted something else, during a discussion about Terence Rattigan and the style in which he should be played one rainy lunchtime. "Do you know how I see you in thirty years' time, Sebastian?"

"No, Lindsay," I said.

"As the Max Reinhardt of Westcliff-on-Sea!" he said triumphantly.

"Nothing wrong with Westcliff. I hear they've got a lovely theatre there," I replied.

I was right, they do have a lovely theatre here.

Thirty years later, I now live in Westcliff-on-Sea and led the successful campaign to prevent it's closure – a campaign that owed much of its success to the welcome and much needed support of fellow Lyric theatre company member Helen Mirren, now Dame Helen, who originally hailed from Westcliff-on-Sea. I've also produced at the Palace Westcliff three times. The most notable production was *The Winslow Boy* written by, of course, Terence Rattigan, with my son Alexander in the title role

– spooky!

Anyway, I digress – back to the '70s!

As we got nearer to opening of *The Seagull,* the crew and stage management started to need to work on the stage, which meant that the company had to go back into a hall to rehearse for a day.

The Irish Club was too far away and would have been impractical anyway as Lindsay wanted to rehearse with as much of the furniture and props as possible, as the company were now getting used to using them. This meant that we needed somewhere much nearer.

They settled on a hall above the synagogue on Dean Street in Soho, about half a mile from the theatre.

We could fit everything into the company manager's (Trevor Bentham's) car. Everything that is except a rather large and heavy chaise longue, which Lindsay insisted on rehearsing with.

Like all good company managers, Trevor kept a wary eye on the budget and was naturally reluctant to hire a van for just one piece of furniture. Lindsay, however, was adamant that it should be there. Trevor refused to hire a van, and we were at an impasse.

Lindsay was the sort-of director who was used to getting his own way, quite rightly in my opinion; therefore, rather than risk an explosion, I decided to intervene.

Having only recently finished work on the farm, and with a masculine ego about the size of the chaise longue, I said, "Hang on a minute, I think I might be able to carry it."

Lindsay said "Don't be ridiculous. It's about half a mile away."

"Let's see what it weighs," I said, and hoisted it on to my back.

It was quite heavy actually, probably just under sixty kilos but I was confident enough in my abilities to make it as far as Dean Street.

"Are you sure about this?" said Trevor. "You'll have to carry it back as well, you know."

By this time the whole company were looking at me with a sort of admiring incredulity so I couldn't really back down at that stage.

"Yes, yes," I said. "I'll be able to manage that OK; don't worry, Lindsay, it'll be there when you need it."

"You see!" said Lindsay triumphantly, "That's the sort of spirit we need in this company!"

After that remark, it was a done deal.

Trevor said to me, "You're going to have to run the rehearsal as well tomorrow. I can't be there because they're bringing the scenery into the theatre and we're going to start lighting; you'll have to set up props, furniture, everything – and prompt, as well." "Fine," I said, having done the same job many times in rep.

Privately, I was more concerned about getting the chaise longue there and back again.

The next day I got to the theatre in good time, ready to transport my burden. I hoisted it on my back and negotiated my way through the stage door into Great Windmill Street and on to Shaftesbury Avenue.

After a couple of hundred yards, it became heavier and heavier and I really started to struggle. I ignored the pain in my legs back, chest and arms, dug deep and ploughed on, with the sweat beginning to pour off me.

I saw Lindsay Anderson coming down Shaftesbury Avenue towards me.

"Good Morning, Sebastian," he said cheerfully. "Hello, Lindsay," I managed to reply.

"You know you look just like the peasant who carried the cross for Jesus on his way to Calvary!"

"Wonderful," I gasped. "If ever they're casting that part I'll let my agent know."

Lindsay laughed happily and strode freely away from me down Shaftesbury Avenue towards the production office.

I eventually reached the synagogue and, with much relief, tipped the chaise longue off my back and stuffed it into the small lift to take it up to the hall. I mentally thanked Jehova that I didn't have to lug it upstairs as well.

The actors duly arrived, the rehearsal came and went without a hitch; I was left with the sofa to transport back to the theatre.

Going back was easier as we were on a slight downward gradient, it's funny how you notice these things when carrying heavy weights!

Night was falling and it was coming on to rain. The nightly parade of Soho denizens were beginning to appear in the streets, alleyways and doorways around Old Compton Street and the gathering of starlings at the end of Shaftesbury Avenue set up their ritual evening screeching; anyone whose worked in the West End at nightfall will recognise the noise.

A female clip joint 'hooker' stared at me and my burden as I was slowly wending my way along with the mild curiosity of someone whose seen most things and is no longer surprised by anything.

I passed Trevor Bentham with his umbrella up and his coat wrapped tightly around him against the wind and rain.

"Well done, Sebastian, don't forget 10 o'clock tomorrow sharp for the technical rehearsal."

"OK," I grunted.

I finally got back to the Lyric Theatre, divested myself of the sofa and made my way across to the Lyric Tavern for a well deserved pint.

The Bed Before Yesterday!

The next day it was in to the theatre for three days of technical and dress rehearsals.

As part of the stage management team, as well as performing, I spent my time doing anything that was needed to help speed the production along to the moment when the curtain rose to a paying audience.

In those days when the demarcation line between jobs in the theatre was a little more blurred, I found myself performing many different tasks: setting props, checking the actor's personal props, cleating flats and moving scenery. I even found myself in the flies 'deading the hemps' (aligning all the ropes to make sure the scenery flies out straight and level) for the quite complicated scene change at the end of the first scene.

This was a 'play within a play' which was set in the woods beside a lake, and then the scene changed to Madame Arkadina's grand living room where the rest of the play took place.

It was crucial to get this complicated scene-change flowing as quickly as possible.

It involved unpinning all of the 'trees' which were flown in and pin-hinged to the stage. Once this was done, a signal would be given to the fly-man who would then fly them out.

The stage for the 'play within the play' would then be trucked off rapidly and then the fly-man would lower in the walls for the living room scene. These would then be cleated together.

Cleating a flat is quite an old skill and requires a lot of practice. Basically, attached to the top of one flat is a long rope, rather like an old fashioned washing line, which hangs down the back of the flat. At the top of the adjoining flat there is a cleat hook, exactly the same as you would see on a sailing boat. In order to join the two flats together you lean the flat with the cleat hook back slightly with your left hand and with a flick of your right hand you throw a loop up the rope and then time your pull down on the rope so that it attaches itself over the cleat hook – a bit like lassoing. The flats would then be pulled together by the rope and tied off as tightly as possible. At this point a stage brace and weights would be attached to keep the flats steady. The fly-man would then tighten the hemps attached to the top of the flats and tie them off in the fly's, thus making the flats as rigid as possible. Considering the flats were eighteen-feet-high this required a skilled stage crew who could do this in one or two attempts as speed was of prime importance during a scene change.

I was one of the crew who had this particular skill of cleating, so I was detailed off for this task during the scene-change.

After a while we managed to get this complicated scene change down to about two minutes and then the curtain would rise to reveal Madame Arkadina's sumptuous living room. Hopefully to appreciative gasps from the audience!

On one occasion, our regular stage carpenter at the Lyric went off on holiday and the carpenter from the Queen's theatre deputised for him.

He very foolishly took the stage crew to the pub on one matinee and the entire crew missed the scene change!

The curtain came down at the end of the scene – no stage crew! I turned to the actors and said, "We don't have a crew."

Joan Plowright stepped forward. "Sebastian," she said, "go up and man the fly's and fly the trees out and the flats in."

I said, "Who's going to cleat the flats together? I'm the only one here who can do it."

Joan said, whilst getting rid of her handbag, parasol and removing her lace gloves, "Just get up into the fly's and stand by."

I hared up the ladder to the fly's and grasped the three hemps, ready to pull up the trees.

Joan and Trevor Bentham organised all of the actors to take the pin hinges out from the trees, thus freeing them to be flown. As soon as they were released, I hauled them up into the fly tower where they hung like stalactites. I then flew in the walls for the living room two at a time so they could be cleated together.

I looked down from the fly's and there was Joan Plowright expertly cleating the flats together, only taking one attempt to cleat each piece of scenery and doing it just a well and as speedily as I or any other skilled stagehand would.

Before we knew it the scenery was all in place and secure.

On a signal from Trevor Bentham, I flew out the tabs and almost slid down the ladder on to the stage to make my entrance with a tray of drinks.

Joan was on stage, criss-crossing back and forward as Madame Arkadina like a ship in full sail as if nothing had happened and the whole of the rest of the performance went by without incident, with the audience completely unaware of the backstage drama that had just unfolded.

I asked Trevor after the performance how long it had taken to do the scene change without the crew.

"Two minutes," he replied airily.

"Amazing," I said. "Wasn't it extraordinary what Joan did, cleating those flats?"

"Yes, well," Trevor replied, "you know, she used to be a stage manager."

"Did she?" I said "Well, what d'ya know!"

I still maintain that doing stage management is a vital part of a young actors' training, as you never know what's going to happen.

Thirty years later, like Joan Plowright, I can still cleat a flat. Rather like learning to ride a bike, once you've cracked it you never forget how to do it.

We settled in to the run of *The Seagull* and a few weeks later started to prepare for our next production, *The Bed Before Yesterday* by the ninety-year-old Ben Travers.

Ben turned up at the read-through and stayed with us through the rehearsal period.

Even though he was ninety years old, he had the infectious enthusiasm of a nine-year-old boy and was incredibly charming with an old world politeness and kindness.

I was particularly interested to meet him as I'd appeared in *Rookery Nook* in weekly rep' and was a big admirer.

I was also fascinated to learn, being a keen amateur student of military history, that he'd flown in the Royal Flying Corps during the First World War.

The average lifespan of one of those pilots when they went in to combat was about six weeks, so we were lucky that he survived to make such a contribution to British theatre.

As an assistant stage manager part of my duties were to look after the old boy and make sure that he had everything he needed.

I was chatting to him one day and he said to me, "Aren't the public lavatories in Piccadily Circus awful!"

I agreed, saying that it wasn't a particularly sensible idea to linger in those loos as in those days they were known as the 'meathook' for reasons that are fairly simple to work out.

Ben replied, "Oh, I used to spend hours in there when I was a small boy."

"Really, Ben?" I said.

"Yes," he said. "They were absolutely fascinating."

"Erm… why?" I asked, not knowing what sort of an answer I was going to get.

"Well, you see," he said, "the lavatory cisterns were made of glass; this meant you could see through them to the highly polished Victorian plumbing, which meant you could see the ballcocks working when they flushed. However, what was most fascinating to me as a small boy was the fact that they'd put goldfish in the cisterns, so that when the cisterns emptied the goldfish would flap around gasping for air, and then when the cisterns filled up again the fish would swim around peacefully as before until the next time the cistern emptied. I used to spend hours in there watching them."

You wouldn't dare do that now, I thought to myself.

What a pity we no longer live in an innocent era when a small boy can spend hours in a public lavatory perfectly safely watching goldfish gasping for air without fear.

The Bed Before Yesterday rehearsals were in full swing.

Again I was understudying a couple of roles carrying out stage management duties and Lindsay gave me a small part to play as a cabbie who dropped off Joan Plowright and her luggage at her house.

Just before the technical rehearsal Lindsay came up to me and said, "Now, Sebastian, about this cabbie… I want you to play him like 'Old Bill', do you know who Old Bill is?"

"Yes, Lindsay," I replied. "He was a cartoon character in the *Wipers Times,* the newspaper that the troops published in the trenches of World War One to amuse themselves. He was a lugubrious character with a large walrus moustache."

"Well done, Sebastian!" said Lindsay, somewhat impressed

at my knowledge. "Well that is how I'd like your cabbie to be, just like 'Old Bill.'"

The technical rehearsal was the following day and I went home that evening plotting what makeup I was going to perform for my facsimile of 'Old Bill'.

I dug up my makeup box and took it into the theatre early and then nipped out for a haircut and had my hair cropped quite close so that I could 'grey' it to make myself look older.

I then went into my dressing room at the very top of the theatre, where the understudies were housed, to put on my intricate 'old man' weekly rep' character makeup.

I'd played loads of old men in weekly rep' and knew just how to do the makeup.

The first thing I did was 'grey' my entire head. Then, I drew on the lines on my face with Leichner sticks which were a deep purple colour and Grey blended together.

In those days I didn't have many existing lines so I had to wrinkle my face to see where they would be one day.

Nowadays, as 'Sir' says in *The Dresser,* "I just deepen what's already there!"

Once those lines were painted on I used a number five Leichner stick, which was a yellowy fleshy colour, to highlight the lines I'd painted to make them look deeper. I then powdered off to blend everything in to make it look as natural as possible.

Then it was time for the 'Old Bill' walrus moustache. I took a long piece of grey crepe hair from my makeup box and stretched it over the hot dressing room mirror light bulb to straighten it. Once it was straight I glued it on with Copydex and trimmed it with a pair of nail scissors.

I surveyed the finished result: I was delighted, not so much 'Old Bill' but very like 'Alf Garnett', which I thought was just as suitable.

I then tried on the costume – a battered old suit covered

with a long gabardine Macintosh and finished off with a cap and goggles, 'Old Bill' being a 1920s cabbie.

I was eminently satisfied with the end result and took it all off and went downstairs to the stage to carry out my stage management duties there.

I didn't want to show Lindsay the end result as I wanted to surprise him on the tech/dress rehearsal that evening when I was sure he'd shower me with plaudits.

The time for the tech/dress rehearsal came and at the interval I rushed upstairs to don costume and makeup, ready for my entrance in the second act.

When it came to our entrance I stood waiting in the wings with Joan Plowright weighed down with all her luggage, suitcase trunks etc., that I was to struggle on to the stage with.

Our cue came and Joan swept through the door; what I didn't realise was that Sir Laurence Olivier (Joan Plowright's husband) and also the female producer for HM Tennant were sitting out front, watching with Lindsay.

I followed Joan on, dragging all the luggage, dropped it down and turned round to face her whipping my cap off in the process in happy expectation of a large tip.

Joan rifled through her handbag and produced a small coin.

I'd decided that I'd characterise somewhat and react as if it was a derisory miniscule amount.

I took the coin and looked at it, bit it, and then gave her an outraged, slow burn, resentful look and 'tutted' in disgust. To illustrate this, I jammed the cap back on my head and glared at her.

I started to get titters from some low individuals out front; I was delighted.

Lindsay shouted from the darkness, "Get Off!"

I thought he was joking and slowly backed away from Joan to more laughter from unidentified individuals out front.

"Get off, Sebastian, get off!" Lindsay shouted again.

By this time I was intoxicated by the laughter from out front and continued backing away from Joan with agonising slowness still fixing her with my outraged glare.

By this time Lindsay was almost screaming, "Get Off Sebastian! GET OFF THE FUCKING STAGE!"

I finally exited, but thought, *Sod it, it's only a tech. I'll make it a false exit!*

I then went back and glared at Joan through the glass panel of the door to renewed laughter from the comedy-seekers out front and more foul expletives from Lindsay.

There was a blind on the door panel which Joan, entering into the spirit of things, promptly pulled down, to big laughs from out front. Encouraged by this, I went across to the window and looked through that instead, fixing her with my lugubrious stare to hysterics from the onlookers and screams of rage from Lindsay.

Rather like one does when one wants to silence a noisy parrot by throwing a cloth over it's cage, Joan then drew the curtains at the window to a round of applause from those pleasure-seekers in the auditorium mixed with apoplectic yelps of rage from Lindsay.

Well that's livened things up a bit, I thought to myself.

As I went by prompt corner Trevor Bentham gave me a very serious look.

Oops! I thought, *Maybe I've gone too far.*

We finished the tech/dress and Trevor called me over to prompt corner.

"Sebastian," he said, "do you realise the producer for HM Tennant was out there watching?"

"No," I replied.

"Well, she's furious, absolutely furious and I think she wants to sack you. Lindsay's out there arguing your case at this very moment."

That sobered me up rapidly.

I promptly went to Joan Plowright's dressing room and tapped on the door.

"Come in," she called.

I opened the door.

Joan Plowright was in there with her husband, Sir Laurence Olivier, who was washing his hands at the sink.

Oh My God, I thought. *It's only Henry V! That's all I need!* Joan said, "This is my husband, Larry. Larry this is Sebastian." I mumbled a hello to him and didn't offer to shake his hand, as he was still washing them.

I switched my attention to Joan.

"Joan," I said. "I'm terribly sorry if I threw you or anything during the tech', but I was only—"

She held up her hand and stopped me.

"Threw me!" she said. " We thought it was great fun, didn't we, darling?" she said to Sir Larry.

"It was… it was indeed," he grinned.

"Oh," I said. "Good, well, I'll say goodnight then." "Goodnight," they both said cheerfully and without rancour. I retreated to my dressing room at the top of the theatre, mightily relieved.

As I was taking off my offending makeup Lindsay came in. "I'm terribly sorry, Lindsay," I said. "It won't happen again." "That's all right," he said. "It was my fault for getting you to play it like 'Old Bill. Erm, on reflection I think it might be better to dispense with the character makeup and moustache."

I manfully hid my disappointment and nodded seriously.

He then fixed me with a piercing look and said. "On the first night, Sebastian, I shall be sitting in the stalls with a loaded Lee Enfield.303 rifle trained between your eyes and if you so much as twitch your hand towards your cap to take it off I shall pull the trigger and blow your head to smithereens! Do you understand me?"

"Yes, Lindsay," I said meekly. "Yes, of course."

"Excellent," he said. "Goodnight," and he then left the room.

Having received and digested my performance notes, I breathed a huge sigh of relief and headed for home.

The Bed Before Yesterday opened without further incident and we settled in to a monthly 'repertoire' situation where we alternated with *The Seagull.*

I think they'd decided that the repertory experiment wasn't going to work as there appeared to be no moves towards adding another production to the programme and we settled into the routine of a normal West End run.

This meant I had most days free and was working in the evenings.

Having ceased my hard labour on the farm I'd started, much to my annoyance, to pile on the weight.

I decided to diet and purchased a 'bullworker' to keep in condition; I also joined a Sunday football team as their goalkeeper.

My days being free, I used to spend a lot of time watching the latest movies in the afternoons and then went off to the theatre in the evening – heaven!

I also used to do a lot of reading, particularly of military history which has always been of great interest to me.

I was browsing in Foyles one wet and windy afternoon when I came across the book, *A Bridge Too Far* – Cornelius Ryan's account of the Battle of Arnhem – which I seized and, having flicked, through decided to purchase.

I went to Valotti's, and over lemon tea and salad proceeded to plough through the book.

I looked on the back cover and it said, 'Shortly to be made into a major movie'.

This I have to get into, I thought, *but how?*

After my meal, I went in to the theatre for the evening's performance.

In the corridor I bumped into Miriam Brickman who had phoned my agent all those months ago, inviting me to attend the audition for this production.

"Oh Miriam," I said, "I've just bought *A Bridge Too Far* from Foyles and it says on the cover that it's shortly to be made into a major movie. I don't suppose you know who will be casting it?"

Miriam looked at me steadily. "I am," she replied.

"Oh," I replied, somewhat taken aback. "Erm, I don't suppose you'd consider me, would you?"

"Let me have a word with Lindsay," she replied. "Keep this under your hat, but the Lyric Theatre Company won't be continuing and we'll be closing in a couple of months, so you might be available. I'll let you know what he says."

I carried on down the corridor feeling very sad that Lindsay's experiment to run a repertory in the West End hadn't worked, yet also quite excited.

The evening's performance came and went and, as I was leaving the theatre, I bumped in to Miriam again.

"I had a word with Lindsay and he said he thinks you'd make a marvellous paratrooper. Sir Richard Attenborough is directing the film and we're holding auditions at the dance centre in Covent Garden next Wednesday, starting at 10am."

"Thanks so much, Miriam," I said. "I'll be there."

As I went to leave, Miriam called me back. "Oh, Sebastian," she said.

"Yes, Miriam?" I replied.

"Lindsay said that you've been terrific on this job and that you've worked really hard; he said that you're good to work with and have a lot of potential, and he said that if you carry on in the same way you've got every chance of doing very well… so keep it up."

I paused at the stage door feeling upset that I couldn't say how highly I valued those words and couldn't reciprocate about how I felt about working with Lindsay, how it had changed the whole attitude to my work and the gratitude I felt for being given the opportunity to be a part of the Lyric Theatre Company 'family', which is what it had been to me for the past nine months.

Instead I just grunted my appreciation in an embarrassed fashion and walked off, allowing the darkness of Great Windmill Street to shroud my emotions.

The news about the company closing soon got around the theatre – nothing to do with me! – and the next few weeks passed like the final furlongs of a horse race, interspersed with a couple of wonderful farewell parties.

The day of the casting for *Bridge Too Far* came and I made my way down to the dance centre in Covent Garden, where it appeared that practically every actor in Equity between the ages of eighteen and thirty-five were in attendance.

We all sat down on the floor and Richard Attenborough stepped forward to speak.

He told us that out of the 300 of us that had attended, he was going to select a company of 100 that would be going out to Holland in two stages of fifty each. He told us that we would receive two weeks of basic military training before depicting all the action sequences in the film, which meant we would need basic military skills and would need to look and act like soldiers.

Our primary task was to replicate the gallant 2nd Battalion of the Parachute Regiment, who had heroically held Arnhem Bridge under the command of the legendary Colonel Frost; however, we would also be playing Polish Paratroopers, soldiers from 30 Corps, German SS and American paratroopers.

As we went through the filming process we would all be given parts to play and they would use us as a kind of rep' company and cast those parts as they came up during filming.

He said that we would receive £125 per week salary plus £50 per week expenses money, which would be paid to us in Dutch

Guilders, free barracks style accommodation and breakfast, supper and tea from the location caterers.

In 1976 that was extremely good money and knowing how long filming can take, it promised to be very rewarding financially, as we would basically be able to send home £125 per week and it would be waiting for us in a nice lump when we came home.

The only stipulation he made was that there were to be no overtime payments.

I thought to myself, *Well, Sir Dickie will have to go to sleep at some point which is when we will be able to get some kip,* so I personally wasn't bothered by that condition at all.

Sir Dickie then got us all on our feet and he told us that we were to file past him one by one where he would look at us and indicate as to whether or not we were going to be one of the chosen 100 to go to Twickenham studios for a final briefing before going to Holland.

I must say that I wasn't used to auditioning like this, I rather preferred to deliver a speech or read a scene; however, I stood up and got in line.

As the line filed past, Sir Dickie he would either say "Thanks very much for coming", which basically meant you'd been 'given the elbow', or "See you in Twickenham", which meant you'd got through.

My turn came and he looked at me straight in the face and said, "Thanks very much for coming!"

I'd been weighed and found wanting! I walked out of the dance centre absolutely devastated, my dreams in tatters. I made my way to the theatre in a haze of disappointment. I bumped in to Lindsay in the corridor and he asked me how I'd got on and I told him.

He was sympathetic and philosophised about what a frustrating and ill-requited profession it can be sometimes.

I thought, *Maybe I'll stick to farming in future; you don't get your hopes up so much.*

Over the next few weeks, however, 'the elastic heart of youth' prevailed and I got over the perceived disappointment and started the search for new jobs and work.

The run at the Lyric would end in about a month and I wanted to get something else lined up as soon as possible.

The phone rang in my digs at the vicarage one morning; it was Bernard my agent.

"Yes, Bernard?" I said.

"Sebastian, you're through to the last 100 at Twickenham and you'll be going to Holland after all!"

I couldn't believe it.

"But Sir Dickie told me that I hadn't got through."

"Well I've just had a call from Miriam Brickman and you're in!"

I put the phone down.

Good old Lindsay, I thought, *and good old Miriam.* I could

only assume that they'd put their heads together and pulled a few strings for me.

It doesn't happen often but when it does it's extremely welcome.

I awoke early on the morning of the call at Twickenham Studios to the sound of many horses' hooves, the squeaking of wheels and the jangling of harnesses.

I leapt up and looked out of the window and beneath me I saw the King's troop of the Royal Horse Artillery resplendent in khaki fatigues and polished gaiters clattering their way up to Hampstead Heath to practise their manoeuvres.

This seemed a fitting presage of the next stage that was to come in my life. After bathing and putting on my best clothes, I boarded the train for the circuitous journey from Hampstead to Twickenham.

Arriving there I followed the stream of other excited young actors to a studio where we sat in eager anticipation of what was to come next.

Sir Dickie took to the stage, flanked by Miriam Brickman and David Tomblin, his legendary first assistant director.

Sir Dickie raised his hand to calm the hubbub and started to speak. He told us that we were the ones chosen to pay tribute with our performances to the extraordinary men who had fought at the Battle of Arnhem.

He said that the budget for the movie was an unprecedented fifty million dollars, which was an extraordinary amount then and that he had a stellar cast lined up, including Sean Connery, Anthony Hopkins, Michael Caine, Gene Hackman, Laurence Olivier, Robert Redford, James Caan, Ryan O Neill, Dirk Bogarde, Liv Ullman, Hardy Kruger, and Maximillian Schell.

This was an incredible array of talent as at that time many of those actors could have carried a movie on their own.

We were to go to Holland and, in another unprecedented move, train for three weeks as infantrymen so as to all the better represent the soldiers who had fought in the battle. This was the first time this had ever been done, though the exercise has since been repeated by Spielberg in *Saving Private Ryan* and *Band of Brothers.*

He then told us that we would be going out to Holland in two waves and proceeded to read the names of the first fifty to go.

He read out the first name. "Sebastian Abineri!" he said.

I had to restrain myself from punching the air with my fist! I sat back in a highly relieved manner and listened to the names of the other actors who were going out with me:

David English
James Wardroper
David Auker
Frank Mughan
Farrell Sheridan
Mark York

Niall Padden
Shaun Curry
Jack Mackenzie
Dan Long
Jason White

There are a lot of other names to add to this list, but those names mentioned above will figure in the adventures to come.

Sir Dickie then showed us the film *Theirs Is the Glory*, a 1940s movie made by soldiers that was a re-enactment of the Battle of Arnhem, which they'd so recently fought in.

When the lights came up he turned to us and said, with tears in his eyes, "We've got to get this right, boys! For those men who fought so bravely and sacrificed so much." He then exhorted us to do our research before going out to Holland, to 'think '40s' and read up as much as we could.

I sat in the pub that evening celebrating alone and mulling over his words. I made my way back to the vicarage wondering whether I was worthy to represent one of the 600 lightly-armed iconic heroes who had held Arnhem Bridge for six days against two armoured SS Panzergrenadier Divisions.

As I opened the front door to the vicarage I looked up and saw the steep stairwell.

The landing was about twenty-five feet above me and the floor below was made of marble.

I mentally challenged myself.

If you don't have the guts to jump from the landing into the hallway then you're not worthy of going, I thought to myself.

It didn't occur to me at the time that if I did jump off the landing, twenty-five feet onto a marble floor the chances were I wouldn't be going anywhere!

At that particular moment in time I was a young, slightly inebriated fool and I stupidly took up my own challenge.

I made my way up to the landing. My goodness, it seemed

much higher from up there than from the floor of the landing. Anyway, no going back; I clambered over the banister rails and hung from them by my arms.

Red on! I said to myself, *Green on…! Go!* (You can see I'd done some research already). I let go, whistled down and thudded into the floor about two seconds later.

I was wearing a brand new pair of leather cowboy boots that were the fashion at the time and which had quite a high pair of heels.

As soon as these connected with the marble both my feet slipped forwards and I took the full impact on my back. Fortunately, my neck muscles were strong enough to prevent my head from whiplashing on to the marble too hard and I lay there, unharmed, but with all of the breath knocked out of me and sobering up rapidly.

I gingerly got to my feet and hobbled off to bed, relieved that I hadn't damaged myself too much.

Lindsay had released me from my contract with the Lyric Theatre Company a few weeks before the end of the run to enable me to get to Holland with the rest of my group.

The morning we were due to leave I sat with my bag packed in my digs waiting for the car to pick me up to take us to Heathrow. I was told I would be sharing this with one other actor who we would pick up on the way.

The cab pulled up and I dashed downstairs and loaded my case into the boot. We then drove to West Hampstead and I saw another equally expectant actor staring out of the window of his flat.

He gave us a brief wave and joined us.

"Hi. I'm Sebastian," I said.

"Hello, mate," he replied with a touch of a Liverpool accent. "My name's Frank."

Frank, later to be known as Big Frank, was a big lad, six feet five inches, and with an imposing physique to boot.

He was an incredibly good-humoured, football-mad nutcase and quickly became one of the lynchpins of the group when we got to Holland.

He was also, much to our envy, incredibly attractive to women but he never let that go to his head.

He once said to me, "Seebo" – (this became my nickname along with 'The Donkey', which I've never been able to fathom). "Seebo… if I was with a girl and some lads came out and started booting a ball about and I was able to hear them, I'd leave

the girl and come out and play footie!"

This to me at the time was an extraordinary admission; I mean, I love football with the best of them but I think I'd finish what we were doing first – it's only polite.

I've often wondered in later life if that's why women object so much when men settle down to watch football on TV, perhaps they sense some perceived threat to their sexuality.

Frank, as it turned out, was actually a very talented footballer: he had played for Liverpool apprentices and could head a ball as hard as most blokes could kick it.

We chatted away amiably on the way to Heathrow and Frank gradually became quieter as we got near the airport.

At Heathrow we picked up our tickets and cleared customs and Frank headed off to the bar.

I was really looking forward to the flight, never having flown anywhere before, and therefore didn't feel the need to fortify myself with strong liquor; anyway, it was only about 10.30 in the morning.

We filed onto the aeroplane and took our seats. Frank was sitting across the aisle from me and had gone a sort of grey colour and was sweating like a horse.

I was sitting over the wing next to a wonderful actor called Christopher Good – he was playing the second-in-command to

Anthony Hopkins, who was playing Colonel Frost the hero of Arnhem Bridge.

The plane taxied down the runway and then with a mighty screech catapulted us into the air at what seemed like a sixty-degree angle; it was absolutely terrifying!

Frank was sitting with his eyes tightly closed, gripping the edge of his seat with white knuckles. I thought he might pull the chair out of the floor.

The plane continued its noisy trajectory for what seemed like forever.

This is all wrong! I thought, *We're breaking all the rules of aerodynamics, the next thing that's going to happen is that we'll run out of momentum and come hurtling down at the same angle!*

The plane levelled off, the seatbelt lights were extinguished and we settled in to the flight.

We hit a bit of turbulence as we cleared the coast, which set my heightened nerves jangling again as the wing started to waggle and vibrate alarmingly.

"Why is it doing that?" I said to Chris Good.

Chris replied drily, "It's designed to vibrate like that, if it didn't the wing would break off."

"Oh," I gulped, and lapsed into a terrified silence.

The stewardesses came round with coffee and sandwiches which we barely had time to finish before the seatbelt lights came on again and we were instructed to prepare for landing at Schiphol Airport Amsterdam.

With a hum and a clunk of hydraulics the flaps came up and we started our descent a damn sight too rapidly for my liking.

Another alarming clunk as the undercarriage came down and then a deafening screech from the engines as the captain employed some reverse thrust to assist our braking; then, with a huge shake and vibration, we were down and hurtling along the runway at diminishing speed towards the terminal.

We finally rolled to a halt.

Thank fuck for that! I thought, and breathed easy again.

We cleared customs at Schiphol and were herded onto a coach to take us to Deventer, a small Dutch town on the River Ijsell which was to be our base for the next six months.

We were met by the cadaverous figure of Jack 'Jacko' Dearlove, who had been detailed off to be our chaperone and moral guardian whilst we were in Holland.

Jack was an ex-Desert Rat who had found his way into the film industry; he could have been a mascot for the Desert Rats, as he did bear a startling resemblance to that particular rodent.

Jack had been given the task of making sure we got to the set on time and didn't succumb too much to the fleshpots of liberal 1970s Holland.

A practically impossible task considering he was looking after fifty young actors of varying sexuality who were raring to be allowed off the leash.

I liked Jack, I think he eventually came to care about us quite a lot; he loved football, was a rabid West Ham supporter, and was constantly counselling us about the dangers of too much booze and local girls.

"Right, you lot," he shouted in his high-pitched cockney voice.

He indicated to an imposing, grim-looking building. "This is where you're going to be staying; get in and grab yourselves a bed, leave your luggage and report back out here in five minutes."

We filed in to what became known as 'the old folks' home which it actually was, the old folk having been moved to a new old folks' home across the square.

It was a bit grim: lino' floors and rows of beds, each with a sleeping bag and pillow. There were about ten beds to each room, just like an army barracks.

I grabbed a bed and put my luggage on it and went back out to the coach.

"On you get," Jack told us, "we're going to get your kit."

It was late afternoon and as the coach drove over the Deventer Bridge; having weaved our way through its picturesque streets and alleys, we passed over the glittering River Ijsell and proceeded through the pretty Dutch countryside dotted with windmills and church spires towards Bujsloo, where there was a large network of warehouses to get kitted out.

We piled out and queued up outside one of the buildings to draw our uniforms.

As we waited a squad of extras dressed as German SS wandered past chattering away in Dutch.

All of a sudden there was a huge explosion, mixed with Anglo-Saxon profanities. We whirled round. An old Sherman tank was being worked on by some special effects guys.

They'd dug a load of old tanks left over from the Second World War out of the Dutch polder and were trying to repair them and get them started for the film.

This particular tank's fuel system was obviously shot because when they tried to start the engine it caught fire and brewed up beautifully like a large torch.

Special effects boys were scattering all over the shop as they distanced themselves from the inferno, to much hilarity and mickey-taking.

They just left it there and let it burn itself out whilst they started work on another tank.

Our queue moved into the warehouse where a couple of wardrobe guys were handing out uniforms.

I walked up and a wardrobe guy looked me up and down and said, "Another fuckin' short-arse," and dumped four sets of uniform's in front of me.

We were given, Parachute Regiment gear together with two

helmets: one British Para and another exactly the same but with the Polish Eagle on it to represent the Polish Brigade.

We were then given the complete infantry uniform for 30 Corps with the British 'Battle Bowler'.

Then, a complete American Airborne outfit, including jump boots and helmet, and finally a complete German SS Panzergrenadier uniform, including helmet and jackboots.

We were given all of the webbing, kitbags, ammunition pouches water bottles to go with each uniform.

We stuffed the uniforms into bin bags, stuck sticky labels with our names on them and loaded them on to the coach.

By now the sun was over the yardarm and we persuaded Jacko and the coach driver to allow us to retire to a small bar for a few 'sherberts'.

We got back to the "old folks home" and surveyed our grim surroundings: old lino' floors, a kitchen/canteen for our breakfasts and a large 'recreation room' which had nothing in it except a worn old carpet and tatty old curtains hanging limply at the large windows.

We were strongly advised by Jacko to get to bed early as we had to get up at 5am the next morning to start our training.

We went back to our various dormitories; there were five of them, each with ten iron bedsteads, thin mattresses and sleeping bags.

They'd obviously decided to employ 'the method' with us and were making our surroundings as uncomfortable and basic as they would have been for soldiers back in 1940. We didn't care, as we reckoned we wouldn't be spending much time there anyway as we'd be either working or out enjoying ourselves, and this was somewhere almost bearable to 'kip' despite having to share with ten other blokes.

We discussed ways of organising a roster, so that when indulging in amorous activity with the locals the dormitory would be vacant.

We settled down to sleep and were woken what seemed like ten minutes later – it was actually about three in the morning – by groaning, shrieks, howls and cackles of laughter. We sat up, startled, and in the gloom could make out a group of lads in German helmets, jackboots and underpants cavorting around the room in the darkness.

Before we could get out of bed to confront these intruders, they switched on our main overhead light and then smashed it! Sending shards of glass everywhere and plunging us back into darkness, they then rushed off with howls of maniacal laughter.

Thus started the first phase of the inter-dormitory wars or, nocturnal 'phantom activity'.

We assumed the intruders were the boys in the room next to ours so we went in the next night and soaked all of their bedding.

The whole 'dormitory war episode' culminated with the phantom shitter! To spare his blushes, I shall not name him; however, one night whilst peacefully slumbering, the moonlight in our room was blotted out by a dark figure.

We gradually woke up one by one and stared at him as he stood swaying in the moonlight.

Piece by piece he divested himself of every item of his clothing – he was obviously pissed as a fart. Once undressed, he proceeded to squat down and squeeze out an enormous turd right in the middle of our floor!

Once he'd finished he then stood up, retrieved his clothing, and stumbled out of the room… he didn't even wipe his bum!

We stared at each other from our beds incredulously, struck dumb by what we had just witnessed.

Dan Long, the body builder, finally spoke… "That's a bit strong!" he said.

"Bloody right," I exclaimed. "Right, tomorrow night we're all going into his room and we'll all take a dump on his floor!" (I assumed this was an escalation of the 'Dormitory Wars')

The next morning we woke up and saw his huge excretion right in the middle of our room.

Mark York said, "Cor, look at the size of that. If you stuck a flag in it, it could declare independence!" He then ran gagging from the room.

The rest of the guys disappeared rapido as well.

I thought to myself, *No one's going to clear this up so it looks like it's down to me!* Anyway, I knew the perpetrator and I wanted to confront him.

I found an old coal shovel and, holding my nose whilst suppressing my gagging reflex, I scraped it off the floor.

It was a very hot summer that year and, in the ninety-degree heat, flies were buzzing round it in tight circles. I took it down to the garden where I knew the guilty party was lying, sweating out his hangover. I approached his pink, sweating body; he was twitching slightly as the alcohol was leaving his system. I moved forward stealthily and placed the humming shovel of his own shit under his nose so that he could smell it.

His nostrils dilated and contracted a few times and he eventually opened his eyes to be confronted by his steaming pile, centimetres away from his nose.

He sat up sharpish. "What the fuck is that!" he exclaimed. "That's yours, that is… it belongs to you!"

"It's not, is it?" he said

"Yes, it's yours," I said. "You left it on the floor of our room last night… don't you know when you're having a shit!"

"No," he said.

"Oh come on," I said. "I don't believe you, you're not a baby! Surely you know when you're having a shit?"

"Not when I'm pissed!" he exclaimed. "I got thrown out of a hotel in Newcastle once for putting one in the wardrobe!"

I looked at him suspiciously, decided to believe him and buried the offending item amongst the rosebushes.

After that, whenever he chatted up a girl we'd make remarks

like, "I wouldn't leave your handbag open, love," or, "Watch it, darlin', or he'll slip one into your purse!'

Anyway, back to our first day's training.

We were awakened by Jacko Dearlove the following morning at 5am with the entreaties, "Get up, you lazy bastards..." "Hands off cocks, feet in socks..." "Get your feet on the floor," etc.

We staggered into showers or into our British Parachute Regiment kit and, suitably attired with scratchy serge shirts, battledress, tin hats, berets stuffed in pockets and tangles of webbing holding small packs, water bottles and bayonet frogs, we queued up downstairs in the canteen for our yummy breakfast, which had been prepared by our bleary-eyed Irish cook Ollie, who'd been sent to us by the catering department.

Ollie was a great footballer, boxer and table tennis player and all-round grade 'A' bloke. A cook he was not.

He used to make the scrambled egg with lard, which gave it the consistency of cheesecake, and the bacon was always swimming in grease, topped off by tinned tomatoes. Every morning he used to run the gauntlet of verbal abuse from fifty guys as he served up the disgusting mess he used to refer to as our breakfast.

"Fucking hell, Ollie, you c**t. I wouldn't give this to my fucking dog to eat!" That sort of thing.

Ollie used to come back gamely at us with his broad Irish brogue. "Fucking get it down your necks, you ungrateful bastards! You're lucky to get anything at all, you useless pricks!" This became our morning ritual which we came to know and love almost as much as we loved Ollie, our game little cook

who very nearly poisoned us all.

I decided to not bother with breakfast and grabbed a cup of tea and went outside to get on the coach to take us to Bujsloo where we would be carrying out our training.

Despite being so early in the morning the sun was hot and

you could tell it was going to be a scorcher of a day. I dragged my tangle of kit on to the coach and sat at the back in the corner by the window. Gradually the other lads filed on too and then the coach lurched off through the narrow streets of Deventer towards the bridge over the gleaming River Ijsell. As we drove towards the bridge we witnessed the construction of period houses being built, with wood and plastic designed to replicate Arnhem Bridge prior to the devastation of the battle.

Obviously the bridge at Arnhem could not be used for filming the original battle scenes, as the surrounding area had been completely rebuilt after the war and bore no resemblance to its pre-war surroundings.

Arnhem Bridge had, however, been renamed John Frost Bridge after the gallant Commanding Officer of the 2nd Battalion Parachute Regiment, who had held it for 6 days in the face of overwhelming odds.

Joe Levine, the producer of *A Bridge Too Far* had found the town of Deventer, which had its own twin-spanned bridge over the River Ijsell and a car park under one end of the bridge. On this car park they were replicating the original buildings, which had clustered round Arnhem Bridge during the battle.

This was to be our primary location for filming over the next six months. We drove over the bridge and onwards into the Dutch countryside towards Bujsloo. They have a very good set of planning laws in Holland, where towns which have a river running through them are not allowed to build on the western side of the river, only on the eastern side.

This means that there is a very good integration between the urban and rural communities in Holland. Very often you'd witness tractors carrying hay or whatever through Dutch towns back to the western side and the two communities are truly integrated, nowhere in Holland will you find the urban sprawl we undergo in the UK.

The early morning mist was rising from the low-lying Dutch

fields as we drove towards Bujsloo, our training camp for the next three weeks.

We arrived at Bujsloo and debussed under the sceptical gaze of a team of stuntmen who'd been brought in to train us.

We were ushered into a large room with a team of hairdressers who proceeded to whip out earrings etc. and then 'short-back-and-sides' all fifty of us. It was very quick, the whole process took about one hour to divest fifty of us of our 1970s flowing locks.

We emerged looking a little, though not much more, like 1940s squaddies. We were then introduced to the team who were to train us.

There was Douggie Robinson, a tough stuntman with steel-grey hair and a solid physique; Paul Weston, a tall, dark and good-humoured stunt guy who later went on to become Superman's body double and he also doubled for Roger Moore in all of his Bond movies; Shaun Curry, an actor who was part of 'Attenborough's Private Army', which from now on is to be referred to as the APA.

Shaun was an ex-battalion sergeant major in the Coldstream Guards; he was to be assisted by two other actors – Jack Mackenzie, an ex-corporal in the Royal Marine Commandos, Mark Sheridan, who was ex-Royal Norfolk's and 'Bill the Armourer', who was to teach us the workings of the English, German and American weapons we were to use. Overseeing the whole process was Colonel John Waddy, the military advisor on the film. John Waddy had fought in the Battle of Arnhem as a Major in 156th Para Battalion, he was wounded twice and taken prisoner; after the war he went on to command the Special Air Service.

There were a couple of other actors in the APA who'd experienced military service: Dan Long, who had a superbly honed physique, was ex-Royal West Kents (The Buffs) and Mark York was ex-Parachute Regiment.

The rest of us had little or no past military experience and were depending on the above individuals to teach us what was required to replicate the men who had fought so bravely thirty-two years before in 1944.

The first job they undertook was to teach us how to make our webbing fit. Basically in the Army they don't care if your uniform doesn't fit you properly, but your boots and webbing have to fit like a glove.

This somehow makes the rest of you look soldierly once your webbing is pulled together and fits correctly it makes everything else look right. So after much fiddling and adjusting, we all put our webbing on and became a tad more like soldiers but we were still a right shower.

We were then given rifles and ordered to line up behind Paul Weston and Douggie Robinson, who proceeded to take us on a two-mile run around Bujsloo lake. The run finished at a huge manmade hill, rather like the location from the movie *The Hill*, which we were to run up one side and down the other, finishing with the completion of a short assault course.

Some actors dropped out halfway round, though not many, and a couple pretended to faint but the rest of us plugged on in the blazing heat.

Having spent many months as a farm labourer and then been on a fitness drive when I was working at the Lyric, I was finding the run reasonably comfortable and maintained second place behind Christopher Good, a tall rangy actor who was playing our second-in-command, Major Cornish. I was breathing down his neck as we came to the hill, and at this point I decided to try and break him on this slope and push in to first place.

I sprinted up the hill past Christopher and ran down the other side where we were to perform a forward roll and then proceed over the assault course.

My ill-fitting helmet had been banging rhythmically on my

head throughout the run and as I approached the forward roll, I took it off and held it in my hand as I carried out the roll.

Colonel Waddy leapt in front of me.

"Put your helmet back on," he ordered me, "then go back and do it again."

I put my helmet back on properly and tightened the chinstrap and then did the forward roll again which meant that about fifteen blokes had passed me by the time I came to the assault course. However, I was the only one who managed to climb the ropes with a full pack and a rifle without using my feet.

I went up hand over hand, just using the strength in my hands and arms, which impressed everybody (I was a bit of a show off then!). We finished the run and lined up, chests heaving and sweating profusely We then had a quick water break.

After that we had to crawl through sand; on the command, "Advance!" we had to get to our feet and sprint forward, and on the command, "Cover!" hit the deck and crawl through the sand again.

This was repeated over and over again for about twenty minutes and was totally exhausting.

This ordeal finally stopped and we were given a tea break where we lay on our packs in the hot sun, drinking tea and smoking.

They soon had us on our feet and we spent the rest of the morning carrying out foot drill and learning how to march.

After lunch we carried out fire and movement training, skirmishing, and learning how to attack pillboxes and blow them up with explosives packs. They certainly kept us moving and after three weeks of this we began to look, feel and even behave like soldiers.

We learnt all of this very rapidly, being actors. It was easy learning the foot drill, rather like learning the steps to a rather 'butch' dance, the uniforms were our costumes so we worked hard making them look right and the Lee Enfield Rifle was our main prop, so we worked to familiarise ourselves with it and learned how to look after it, clean it, and take it apart.

And as for behaving like soldiers, that was us 'getting in to character'. Or maybe it's not that difficult to get any group of young men to behave like soldiers when you look at the millions who they trained for the First and Second World War.

All of the weapons on the film were 'practical', i.e. real and working weapons, and were kept in a large arms truck under the eagle eye of Bill the Armourer – a tough, hatchet-faced ex-Army veteran who worked for Bapty's, the weapons hire company, in London.

There were thousands of real British, German and American rifles and machine guns on this truck.

The local police were very worried that it might get hijacked by the South Moluccan terrorist group, who were operating in Holland at the time, as there were enough weapons on this truck to equip a small army.

We were informed in no uncertain terms that if we lost our weapon we would be sacked from the film and sent home.

This was known as a 'KLM Job' (after the Dutch Airline that had brought us here).

Whilst we were training, we weren't allowed to go out in the evenings and sample the local nightlife, which was probably a good idea.

That meant that at the end of three weeks of early nights, long days of hard training and no alcohol, we were all getting pretty fit.

The embryonic hub of a football team began to emerge and evenings before darkness fell were spent in the square outside the the old folks' home thumping a ball about in our army boots. The natural process of selection whittled the fifty of us down to a fairly reasonable squad of about fifteen players, which we decided to form a team from and challenge all comers.

I was designated as goalkeeper.

On the final day of our training, we were lined up in front of Colonel Waddy, who delivered the following message to us.

He said that at the beginning of the training process he would never have believed that a group of actors could possibly have come anywhere near simulating the men who had fought at Arnhem. He said that we had achieved more in two weeks than it would take the average recruit to learn in three months, that a lot of us were officer material and if this were for real woe betide any enemy we were put up against!

Well you can imagine this made our heads swell enormously!

Personally, I didn't quite believe it myself, as I felt we had a long way to go before we came anywhere near that standard. Wise old Colonel Waddy was doing the classic trick of giving us a huge psychological boost so that we had the right level of confidence and natural 'swagger' in front of camera that was required to replicate the original men who had fought at the battle. However, to quote *Henry V*: "All things are ready if our minds be so!"

We were then given red berets and allowed to march through Deventer for the two miles to the production offices.

Looking back, this was a huge honour, as in that part of Holland the British Parachute Regiment were revered, quite rightly, for the heroism they had shown whilst attempting to liberate the Dutch in the terrible Battle for Arnhem Bridge.

We enjoyed the applause and cheers from the local Dutch populace on the march, however, we arrived feeling like frauds. This feeling was made worse by the congregation of the "chippies" – British carpenters who had been brought over to build the gliders and carry out the construction work around the bridge – who, alerted by the noise of our reception, slowly gathered outside their workshops and started to 'take the piss' out of us.

Shaun Curry, our sergeant major, instructed us to, "Keep your eyes to the front… Don't react… Show them you don't give a fuck… Stand fast and bollocks to them." This was all said out of the side of his mouth as he scuttled up and down behind our stationary ranks like a mother hen.

We endured the shouted comments of, "You're not real soldiers, you're just a bunch of 'max factors'(actors)", and, "What a bunch of poofs. My bird's tougher than you lot".

They stopped when Sir Dickie came out to inspect us and congratulate the training team for the job they'd done, but they started again once he'd gone back into the offices.

We endured this in silence and maintained our discipline because of the growled exhortations of the actors performing the roles of our NCO's who ordered us not to react. They'd all been in the Army for real and knew the form.

This tactic actually started to work as the mickey-taking comments began to subside due to the fact we were standing like a stonewall and not reacting at all.

We were given the order to right turn and march away. David Auker started to sing the old Army refrain 'Colonel

Bogey'; we immediately got the message and when it came to the line '*Himmler is pretty Simmler*' we all weighed in with, "*BUT POOR OLD CHIPPIE'S HAVE NO BALLS AT ALL!*"

The next night we were allowed of the leash and went for a drink. Some of our guys went straight to the bar the chippies used and had a monumental 'punch up' with them. Even Ollie our

cook joined in.

The fight started in the gents', went up the corridor into the bar and then out into the street. They never 'took the piss' out of us again and after that we all got on like a house on fire.

We then started work on filming in earnest.

In the film there is a sequence where the Paras get to the Bridge and then Colonel Frost decides to take out a German pillbox halfway across.

In order to replicate this sequence Colonel Waddy, our Military Advisor who had been at the battle, selected twelve of us to re-enact this engagement.

Waddy treated it like a real mission in that we rehearsed intensively for it – rather like putting on a play!

We spent a couple of days rehearsing skirmishing forward, hitting the deck on the hard concrete and then retreating carrying our casualties with us.

He then sat us all down in front of a blackboard at the old folks' home with a chalked diagram of the bridge with the pillbox halfway across.

He started to speak: "Right, I'm dividing you into three sections of four men each. Section one will go up the eastern cycle track, section two up the main road, and section three up the western cycle track. The pillbox is there (pointing with his stick) and the fucking Krauts are at the other end of the bridge." This got an uneasy laugh until one of the more politically correct amongst us put up his hand and said, "Colonel, those

people you refer to as fucking Krauts are now our allies."

Waddy replied, "They may be our allies… but they're still fucking Krauts!"

This got a big laugh and rather 'set the tone' for the rest of the shoot.

The day for filming the sequence arrived we got to our start positions on the bridge facing the pillbox which housed Bill the Armourer with an MG42 Spandau belt-fed machine gun and a 'number two' to help feed the rounds into the breech.

I was in section two going up the main road and the pillbox was on the pavement of the western cycle track.

I decided to treat it for real and suggested to my companions in my section that if the MG42 opens up and pins us down to hug where the kerb of the pavement met the road and crawl forward using it as just a little bit of cover.

My reasoning was that the machine gunner would be concentrating more on the lads rushing forward. It might be harder, and also more time-consuming, for him to depress his barrel and take those of us crawling forward out; I thought that it might give us half a chance to get close enough to rush the pillbox and, if he did focus on us, it may draw fire from the other lads.

If it had been for real the only chance we'd have had would have been for the MG42 to jam, which unfortunately didn't happen which was fatal for 2 Para when they did do it for real.

The commands from the unit came: "Standby… Rolling… Speed… ACTION!"

We started to move rapidly towards the pillbox after about ten seconds the MG42 opened fire on us with the sound like a malevolent sheet tearing such was the rate of fire.

I hurled myself down by the kerb and crawled forward; I got to within ten feet of the pillbox and jumped up and leapt over the rail on to the western cycle track to find myself staring straight down the barrel of the MG42 as it opened fire I could feel the hot air from the barrel and the splinters of wood hitting me as the shredder in the barrel ground up the wooden bullets going through it… I was well and truly 'brown bread' as Bill the Armourer, who was operating the MG42, took great pleasure in telling me later!

This marked the start of filming with every subsequent day as eventful at the preceding ones.

There have been reports that the birth rate in the region shot through the roof in the months after we left and then settled back down again afterwards to its' normal level.

Whether that was true or not I don't know but it really wouldn't surprise me if it had been the case.

We soon settled down to the routine of filming in the blazing heat of the day from 7am in the morning; it was the summer of '76 and it was so hot cows were dying in their fields.

We had a wonderful time; impeccably turned out girls arrived, as if by magic, from all over Northern Holland with condoms stuffed in their handbags in their pragmatic Dutch liberal fashion. A lot of them 'bent over backwards' to help us have a wonderful time in the bars and clubs to the strains of Abba – '*Can You hear the guns Fernando*'!

FOOTBALL!

Our football team was coming on nicely. We had fifty guys to choose a squad from and some of the players were quite useful: Big Frank, our striker, had played for Liverpool Apprentices and David English had played as a professional apprentice; a couple of other guys had had trials for Brighton and Hove Albion of all teams! Another had played at county level and the rest of us had all made our School First 11's.

The first thing we needed was football kit. None of us had thought to bring our football boots with us and we were pondering as to how we would solve this problem when David Auker rushed in, thereby interrupting the constant ping pong tournament that used to go on all day from dawn till dusk in the games room whenever we had a day off which was normally on the weekends. "Lads, lads… there's a deal going at the local sports shop where they say they'll kit the whole squad out with football boots for a fiver each!" (This was the '70s by the way).

We all grabbed our guilders and followed David down to the 'deal' he'd found.

Sure enough, there they were, a pile of perfectly decent footie boots which we all tried on and selected our sizes. Everyone was equipped with a pair except our star player, poor old Big Frank, who at 6'5" and with size 14 feet was sitting surrounded by discarded pairs of boots desperately trying to find a pair that would fit.

I joked that he should play one of the ugly sisters in *Cinderella* when we got back to normal and working in Panto', which didn't go down particularly well with him at the time.

There was a pair that would fit, which were absolutely superb but were way out of his price range and were not subject to the 'deal'. We tried to find another pair that were cheaper, no luck.

We all looked at each other and came to a mutual decision: we put in the equivalent of a couple of quid each and purchased the 'posh pair' and gave them to him.

Big Frank looked at us, his eyes glistening and clearly moved. "You'd do this for me, lads…? I won't forget this, I promise." "That's all right, mate. Just make sure you score loads of goals with them," was the general attitude. "Anyway, you're our

captain, can't have a captain with no boots."

He was our best player: no Big Frank meant no team!

We had a few practice matches in the square outside the old folks' home – not in our new boots, but our army boots – and settled on a team. I was elected as goalkeeper, Big Frank was centre forward and our target man, as he was brilliant with his head, and he formed a partnership with David English, an extremely skilful player who played wide on the left.

One of our tactics, which worked quite well on occasion, was me clearing the ball from the penalty area on to Big Frank's head, who'd drop back to just over the halfway line and flick it to David English. He'd bring it down the left wing and cross it on to Frank's head, who by now was in the opposing penalty area who more often than not would get a header on target.

Pretty basic stuff, but sometimes quite effective.

After a few practice matches, we challenged the film crew to a match.

They accepted with alacrity as they had about 300 to choose a team from and had some pretty good players working with them.

We settled on an afternoon at about 3pm, after having cleared it with Dave Tomblin, the first assistant director, and Sir Dickie who loved football and was on the board at Chelsea.

The highly anticipated day of the match came and during filming at about lunchtime David Tomblin turned to Sir Dickie and said, "Don't forget the match this afternoon, Dickie."

Sir Dickie said, "Oh my God, we must get down to the ground." He then picked up David's loudhailer and shouted, "Right, that's a wrap, everyone. Transport will be leaving the unit base in half an hour to take everyone down to the ground."

I can't think of any other film director who would wrap a multimillion-pound movie halfway through the day for a friendly football match!

We arrived at the football ground and headed for the changing room; as I was getting changed into my goalie's strip I was accused by the other lads of wearing the same pair of underpants for the past six weeks.

They were yellow Y-fronts with blue piping.

"Nooo," I said. "I went to Marks and Sparks and bought four identical pairs of these before I flew out here. Surely you've noticed the other three pairs hanging on the washing line outside the old folks' home, washed in the brand new machine so kindly provided for us by Anthony Hopkins (who was playing our C/O Colonel Frost)."

They insisted that they hadn't seen them and carried on with the calumny that I'd been wearing just one pair for six weeks on the trot.

I treated this as typical light-hearted 'boys' pre-match Footie banter and basically ignored it and tried to focus on the match ahead.

Anthony Hopkins took his commanding officer role quite seriously, he'd also managed to acquire for us a table tennis table, which was used constantly. Less useful was an old, out-of-tune upright piano which was only ever played at around 3am in the morning by some pissed-up member of the APA and sounded awful, though no doubt beautiful to the drunken instrumentalist at the time.

Anthony Hopkins was waiting outside to 'kick off ' the match against the unit.

Jacko Dearlove, our ex-Desert Rat and West Ham-supporting chaperone, opened the door of the changing room. "Come on, lads, kick-off time." He started to give us a pre-match team talk: "Frank, don't forget to drop down when Seebo (me) clears the ball and flick it over to Dave English and motor up into their penalty area. Seebo, remember to stay on your line when they cross or have a corner; they've got a couple of tall guys who'll make mincemeat of a short-arse like you."

I got into my goal and warmed up with a few practice shots. The ref blew his whistle and called the two captains together to 'toss up'; we stayed as we were and Anthony Hopkins came on to the pitch to kick the game off.

I was standing on my goal line, ready for the game to start, when I was engulfed with an inferno of sound. There was a blinding flash and the whole world went dark as I was surrounded by soot and dust. My hearing was reduced to just a high-pitched ringing sound which took ages to clear, rather like Tom Hanks at the beginning of *Saving Private Ryan*. As the dust settled and my hearing began to resemble just a small semblance of normality, I was aware of much hilarity from the touchlines as the spectators, including Richard Attenborough and Miriam Brickman, were falling about with laughter. It dawned on me that the special effects boys responsible for all the explosions in the film had booby-trapped my goal line with a very special explosives mix. I played the rest of the game with a blackened face and covered in soot.

They're not taking this seriously, I thought.

I was soon disabused of that thought as it became apparent, once the laughter had subsided, that they intended to take this match very seriously indeed.

They really didn't want to lose this match to a bunch of 'max factors'! And fairly quickly they began to outclass us, but not by much. I was forced into action almost from the beginning of the match and was kept very busy throughout the game. Poor old Olly, our gallant cook, was playing full back and saved my arse on many occasions. As the unit team surged forward, I managed to pull off a few desperate saves and we endeavoured to keep them at bay for the first twenty minutes or so.

One of their forwards was getting very frustrated by Olly, who was snapping at his heels like a heroic Irish Terrier. He got so fed up with this that he turned, lifted Olly up by his shirt front and slapped him right across the face! Well, I wasn't having that, so I chased him down to the touchline and, right in front of Dickie Attenborough and Miriam Brickman, I roared, "You c**t!" And let fly at him with a swingeing haymaker.

For some reason, it didn't connect as intended, as I found myself flying backwards through the air. Big Frank, having divined my intentions, had grabbed me by the back of my jumper and hauled me back just as I let fly with the words.

"Pack it in, Seebo, you'll get sent off… get back in goal." I obeyed my captain and thus avoided being sent off.

We got to half time 2–1 down, Big Frank having scored using our tactic – clearance from me onto his head on the halfway line, a flick on to Dave English who motored up the left flank and crossed it on to Big Frank's head who slotted it in beautifully.

The unit had got the measure of us in the second half and we finished the game 5-2, much to my annoyance as I had let in five goals in our first match. I wasn't happy, but was assured by my kind team mates that it wasn't down to me, as our defence had been penetrated much too often and I'd been flying around our goalmouth like a cat in a washing machine!

The game was designated a huge success and the actors and crew got on really well; we all became good mates. There was some talk of combining the two teams and taking on the local professional side, Deventer Go Ahead Eagles, in a charity match. Sean Connery was keen to play as he used to kick around with us every lunchtime.

I wrote to the club floating the idea, but they didn't fancy risking half their squad being injured by a bunch of enthusiastic amateur 'cloggers', as they assumed we'd be – we weren't, we were better than that – and the film unit weren't too happy at the prospect of Sean Connery possibly breaking his leg. The whole idea never really got off the ground – pity!

We got better and played a few more games against the local fire brigade and the nurses (male) from the local hospital, and then another game against the unit who thrashed us 5-1! My excuse was that I was quite badly injured, having fallen off a wall before the match and consequently put my hip out – it still gives me a bit of trouble on damp mornings – and chipped a bone in my arm… that's my excuse and I'm sticking to it!

Anyway, I got better and as actors were featured and sent home more and more spaces became available at the old folks' home where we were billeted.

We were assured that our football team was safe from being sent home because we had basically prevented a huge disaster from happening by putting out a fire in one of the houses constructed of plastic and wood which had caught alight.

What happened was that we were filming the Para's repelling Grabner's charge, where Hauptmann Paul Grabner tried to dislodge 2 Para by punching across the bridge with an armoured column. We were firing Lee Enfield's, Sten's, Bren PIAT's etc. and, to give the effect of battle, the special effects boys had metal containers which were permanently alight and giving off columns of smoke. Anyway, one of these got too hot and set fire to the tar on the roof of the building we were occupying and the whole roof went up quite rapidly. We were ordered to evacuate as there was 5,000 gallons of petrol in jerrycans stored in the building to the fuel the vehicles.

We picked up our weapons, as we'd been trained to do, and beat an orderly retreat down the stairs. The location was surrounded by Dutch onlookers and one of them said, quite loudly, "Ha ha ha. The British run away!"

We looked at each other, resplendent in Second World War Parachute Regt' kit with red berets, and collectively thought, *Fuck That*! We left our weapons in the charge of some boys from the crew and went back up to tackle the blaze – I don't know what we thought we were going to do as we had no fire fighting kit but we were going to try. Anyway, we got back on to the roof and Niall Padden noticed a big water tank on legs on the roof! We got behind it and basically pushed and shoved and the whole thing toppled over and washed across the roof with a big *whoosh*, thus extinguishing the flames!

Dickie Attenborough rushed up to the building in a Tiger tank with his head poking out of the turret and Dave Tomblin sitting on it with him.

"Well done, boys," he exclaimed. "David, take all their names and make sure they all stay out till the very last day of filming!" Dave Tomblin then proceeded to take our names, eleven of which were the APA footie team!

We resumed our positions on the extinguished roof, happy in the knowledge that we were staying out till the end of the shoot and that we hadn't let down the reputation of the Parachute Regiment in front of the Dutch.

There were now around twenty of the original fifty who first came out to Holland, which meant there were quite a few spare beds.

I was sitting in the games room of the old folks' home one evening and David Tomblin walked in with a couple of tough-looking lads who were about our age. It turned out they were members of 1 Para who'd come out to film the jump sequences. They fancied doing some extra work, as they had a long leave due and quite fancied the twenty-quid-a-day extra's fee, plus the free kip, grub etc. and a chance to fraternise with the local Dutch girls and associated nightlife… and of course they didn't need training. David said, "This is Seb," indicating myself. "He'll show you where you can kip and where everything is, the call sheet for the next day will go up on the noticeboard in the hall every night. Make sure you're on time or we'll send you home… Seb, this is Tony and this one's Jim. Seb will show you where you can kip and where the showers and the canteen is – he'll look after you.

And fucking behave yourselves."

As an ex-Royal Marine Commando, David knew what the Para's could be like – almost as bad as us!

I showed them where to kip, listened to their stories about near misses on their jumps and established that they both played for the Battalion Football Team… interesting.

A few days later a couple of fresh-faced public schoolboys arrived, who had somehow blagged themselves on to the shoot as extra's. They'd joined their combined cadet force at school and so knew all about weapons, skirmishing etc. They fitted in rather well and were also good footballers.

As for behaving themselves, they were worse than us and the Para's put together! But they somehow got away with it, as they were quite charming and spoke posh! That gets you a long way in life!

After a few practice footie sessions, a germ of an idea fermented about taking on the unit again in one last match.

We put the idea to the unit, who jumped at the idea, as they quite fancied thumping us again. I then approached the team committee – basically Big Frank and Dave English – about dropping four of our guys and including the new four additions to our strength.

Frank didn't like the idea much, as he didn't want to upset four of our mates, so he said, "All right, Seebo. I don't like it, but if you want to do it you'll have to take over as captain because I don't want to have to tell them they're out."

I thought about it and came to the conclusion that you 'can't make an ommelette without breaking a few eggs' and told our four lads they weren't playing the next match. I deliberately chose the least enthusiastic players and they actually took it quite well.

I made a couple of changes to our team formation, putting the two Paras in midfield. I moved Dave English, who was a skilful player from left wing to inside left, putting one of the public school boys on the left wing, and James Wardroper on the right wing, with the other public school boy at inside right.

I then said to the unit, who were taking the mickey a bit, that they weren't going to win.

"What d'you mean? Of course we are!"

"No, you're not… because I'm not going to let any goals in this time!"

This was picked up by the head of props, the lovely old Jack Towns

"What are you talking about, Seb? You've let in ten in the last two games!"

"Not next time," I replied.

"Here's £20 in guilders that says you will," said Jack. "Taken," I replied.

I had to keep a clean sheet now or that would be half my week's expenses gone.

The unit had heard about the new additions to our squad

and brought in a couple of new guys themselves: one lad who'd played for Queen's Park Rangers and another who was on the books at Scarborough United, a good semi-pro team.

The day of the match arrived; it was a morning kick-off with perfect playing conditions during a rare cool spell, with a drop of rain the night before making the pitch eminently playable.

We were playing at a local Dutch football club with a car park, clubhouse and railings round the pitch behind which stood about 300 spectators. Word had spread and a lot of people were keen to watch the eagerly awaited 'deciding' match.

All the usual people were there: Dickie Attenborough, Dave Tomblin, the stunt boys, the crew and visiting mates, families, girlfriends etc., so there was quite a buzz going around when we kicked-off.

This time it was our turn to surge forward and the unit didn't know what had hit them.

Our new team seemed to be gelling extremely well and we were all over them like a cheap suit. For the very first time I had relatively little to do in the first forty-odd minutes and at half time we were 2-0 up!

We went into the changing room and Big Frank said, sweeping the fringe from his eyes, "We've got 'em beat, lads... they're fucking shitting themselves every time we go forward! Keep playing like this and we'll beat the bastards!"

I concurred, thinking that if we carry on like this I'd be taking twenty quid off Jack Towns.

The second half started with a new addition to the unit team: a square, ginger-headed attacking midfielder who made it his business to harass me every time I collected the ball.

Eventually, I turned to him and said, "If you don't fuck off, you ginger c**t, I'll pull your fucking head off!"

He turned and looked at me, with an expression I sort of recognised, and trotted off without saying anything in return.

Dave Auker said, as I went to clear the ball, "D'you know who that was?"

"No." I replied.

"That was Dickie Attenborough's son, Michael!"

Oh shit! I thought to myself, *You've got to keep an eye on your networking even in the heat of a football match!*

After I finished on *Bridge,* Michael gave me a job at the Leeds Playhouse, so he obviously didn't hold it against me.

It was now halfway through the second half and the score was still 2-0. The unit had again begun to get the measure of our new formation somewhat and were pressing hard; I was forced on several occasions to play out of my skin but was still managing to keep a clean sheet… just.

The ball bounced off David Auker for a corner to the unit. Their player from Scarborough was lining up to take it when Jack Towns pulled out a handful of guilders and waved them at me. "That's yours after the game, son!" he shouted.

"Put them away, Jack," I shouted back. "The game's not over yet."

"Don't worry, mate," he replied. "That's your money… you've played a fucking blinder!"

The ball floated across – a perfect corner. The new unit player from Queen's Park Rangers hung in the air like an angel. How he stayed there for so long I'll never know… The ball skidded off his head into the bottom corner of my goal coming off the post as it did so. I desperately tried to stop it, nearly knocking myself out on the goalpost, but there it was, nestling in the corner of the netting – 2-1.

Right, all bets are off, I thought to myself, *let's just concentrate on keeping it at 2-1.*

From then on it was real end-to-end stuff. As Shakespeare would have said, 'First one better then another best, both struggling to be victors breast to breast!'

In the dying minutes after I'd pulled off a save that I still can't understand, the unit put in a long, desperate clearance which came looping slowly to Dave Auker.

"Trap it, Dave, and boot it into touch!" I screamed hoarsely. He didn't... he took a long punt at it and missed it completely. The player from Scarborough danced round him with the ball and tapped it to the guy from Queen's Park Rangers. I desperately came out to narrow the angle, but to no avail – he simply drilled it past me and into the net for 2-2.

The final whistle went as I was picking the ball out of the net. The 300 crowd erupted, our two teams congratulated each other. Honours Even was the general consensus, Steve Lanning said, "That was the most exciting match I've ever watched. It

wasn't the best match... but it was the most exciting."

I showered off and went into the bar of the clubhouse. I pulled out my guilders and proffered them to Jack Towns.

"Fuck off," he said, and handed me twenty quid. "I'm not taking it, Jack," I said. "You won the bet."

Neither of us would take each other's money, so we both put it in to a 'kitty' and used it to get roundly pissed! Most satisfactory! Especially as £20 then was worth around £153 in today's money!

Cricket or the reincarnation of the rabbit

PATIENT: "Doctor, Doctor! I've got a cricket ball stuck up my arse and all me mates are taking the piss out of me!

DOCTOR: "You've got a cricket ball stuck up your arse? How's That?

PATIENT: "Now don't YOU fucking start!"

That is my favourite cricket joke by a mile I'm sure Dave English has heard it before, however.

The reason I relay it is because something similar happened to Dave Auker in that he spent about a month on the shoot wandering around with what looked remarkably like a cricket ball stuck in his hand.

We were having a 'nutty half hour' in the old folks' home with table tennis going on, someone playing the piano and me trying to write a letter home to my family.

All of a sudden the door flew open and in lurched Dave Auker with a long piece of 'drool' hanging from the corner of his mouth, a German helmet on his head, an Afghan coat turned inside out, a pair of steel-rimmed specs and a pair of lederhosen (leather German shorts with braces). A pink, sausage-shaped draught excluder was shoved up the side and banged against his knees like a long pink penis that had escaped it's boundaries.

We all got mildly hysterical over this and Dave decided to show Norman.

"I must show Norman," he exclaimed and rushed upstairs to Norman's room, with us all following. Norman, however, was 'otherwise engaged' in the room with his Dutch girlfriend.

Auker barged through the door into his room with us all close behind. The girl, seeing Dave drooling with his pink 'penis' swinging and with us all behind him, let out a gargantuan scream of alarm!

Norman leapt out of bed and smacked David in the mouth really hard, turning the long stream of 'drool' into an interesting pinky red colour.

David turned from a rampaging loon into an angry bull (he was an extremely powerful bloke).

"You c**t, Norman!" he shouted, and let fly with an enormous right hook which, if it had connected, would probably have taken Normans' head from his shoulders.

Norman wisely ducked and Dave's fist drove into the doorpost of Norman's room where it made a sickening 'cracking' noise.

David hopped about cradling his shattered fist, cursing Norman and calling all sorts of plagues onto his head.

We'd all stopped laughing by this time and were working out how to get him to hospital.

I'd recently purchased a used Citroen 2CV, so I bundled Dave into that, after having removed the pink draught excluder, and took him to casualty.

We walked in and the nurses, upon seeing Dave in his outlandish outfit, weren't quite sure which department to send him to. I think their initial instincts were to direct us to the psychiatry department; however, upon seeing his hand they took him away to sort him out whilst I waited in reception.

A few hours later he returned with what looked like a cricket ball bandaged into the palm of his hand as a splint.

"I've got to keep it there for about two months!" he said miserably.

I attempted to look sympathetic, whilst trying not to laugh. When we got back on set the crew barracked him mercilessly about this. There was no question of sending him home, they

were having far too much fun 'taking the piss'.

Every day there were cries of, "Nice catch, Dave"... "Well held"... "Howzat!" etc.

David endured this for a couple of months in a good-humoured way. However whenever a cricketing simile flew through the air, David English used to stiffen and almost 'sniff the air' like a well-trained Pointer Dog.

The more he heard "Owzat!" and "Well held", the more tense and excited he became until he eventually resembled a Greyhound, trembling with anticipation!

Eventually he cracked and walked on to the set one morning with a cricket bat, a real cricket ball and a set of portable stumps... goodness knows where he got those in the middle of Holland.

He rapidly organised us into a cricket team where we had impromptu matches either on set amongst the rubble or in the square outside the old folks' home after work.

When we started our basic military training on the film, it was decided to give us a training course on gun safety to be run by Bill the Armourer.

One morning Bill walked in with a dead rabbit, hung it up on a tree and told us to gather round.

"Right," he said. "Now I'm going to show you the damage a blank round can do to you."

We had two types of blank ammunition: a bulleted blank, a round with a wooden bullet that they used to use with the machine guns that had a shredder on the barrel to grind the bullet into small wooden splinters, and a crimped blank with no projectile in it.

"Never put a bulleted blank into a rifle," he said. "Because this is what will happen."

He then got us to stand back and walked around twenty paces from the rabbit; he took aim and fired, driving a whacking great hole through the rabbit's torso.

Dave English started and exclaimed in horror.

Bill then ejected the round and put a blank crimped round into the rifle.

He then walked up to the rabbit put the barrel beside the rabbit's head and pulled the trigger; the rabbit's eye popped out of its head and on to the side of its face.

Poor old Dave almost fainted and couldn't stop talking about the horror of this event for weeks!

I mean, to me, who had spent many years in darkest Suffolk, one less rabbit in the world didn't mean much… at best it made a nice pie.

To David however the rabbit became like an alter ego. Dave, after all, had many rabbiting characteristics – not the least of which was the facility to rapidly 'mount' many females, which he used to do often, much to the admiration and incredulity of the rest of us. My apologies for any hurt politically correct sensibilities… mind you, if you'd been worried about those you'd have slung this book into the bin many pages ago!

The cricketing drama culminated during the filming of the mass drops by the 1st Airborne Division into Arnhem.

We all drove to Ginkel Heath just outside Arnhem where

the drops had taken place in 1944 and joined around 2,000 Dutch extras dressed as British Para's. They had all brought their own lunch with them and the catering crew gave us all packed lunches in boxes containing two cold pork chops, crisps, a bread roll, Mars Bars, etc.

We all had German uniforms and weapons, as the APA were supposed to represent the German SS who were occupying large parts of the drop zone when the 1st Airborne Division jumped.

We collected our weapons, which included around a dozen MG42 spandau machine guns and deployed ourselves around the perimeter of the drop zone.

How are they going to film this? I thought to myself, *There are over 2,000 extras here spread across around 500 acres of heathland with around fifty aircraft shortly to arrive overhead, where they were going to disgorge around 600 Para's from the 1st Battalion of the Parachute Regiment.*

The APA were dispersed in small groups of about ten men each around the edges of the drop zone and they were to replicate the German response to the mass drop by engaging the Para's as they floated down with small arms and machine gun fire.

Colonel Waddy was in charge of the APA on that day and explained to us what was going on.

"There are around twenty-seven cameras covering this sequence. If you look carefully you'll be able to see them in 'hides' in ditches, up trees etc. There'll be cameras on the wings of the plane and around five stunt cameramen are jumping with helmet cameras.

At around lunchtime we heard over loudhailers, "Aircraft are in the air. Two minutes to go; stand by for 'action.'"

The air started to throb as fifty Dakota propellers beat the sky the aircraft came into view with their doors open with what looked like little baby paratroopers standing by for the order to jump.

Over the loudhailers came the stentorian command, "Action… Action… Action!"

We stood there transfixed, gazing skyward as the Para's jumped with the Dakotas looking like big mummies, each one giving birth to around fifteen little baby Para's with their static lines fluttering like umbilical cords as the planes threw out around 600 tiny warriors.

We watched anxiously, praying that there were no malfunctions, when we heard Colonel Waddy shout, "Don't just stand there staring at them! Fire… Fire… Fire!"

We remembered what we had to do and opened up with everything we had.

The Para's weren't expecting this and as they descended they began to look more and more like human beings and not little toy soldiers any more.

I remember one bloke, who later turned out to be an officer in the Sherwood Foresters Regiment on attachment, who was floating down around twenty yards from me. He stared at me anxiously in the eyes whilst I carefully took aim with my Mauser rifle and pulled the trigger. As I fired he gave a little involuntary movement as if expecting to be hit.

The Para's hit the deck and disappeared!

I thought, *Oh Shit, we're going to be on the sticky end of a counter attack in a moment!*

The unit shouted, "Cut!" and I put my rifle down and went forward to say 'Hello' to them and make sure they were OK. As I went forward one of the Para's, upon seeing my German uniform, said, "Let's 'ave him and round the day off properly!"

I told Colonel Waddy this later and he said, "What did you do?"

"Nothing," I said. "The only thing I did was a hot turd which slid down my trouser leg and into my jackboot!"

He seemed to find this inordinately amusing, so amusing that he threw his head back and laughed uproariously… It probably appealed to his warped ex-SAS sense of humour.

We were invited to watch the 'rushes' for the sequence a couple of days later, which we were all looking forward to. Dickie was very happy, apart from when an airborne camera came down with a parachutist and filmed Dave English, who'd organised his team into an impromptu cricket match. It captured them all on film keeping wicket, smacking the ball into the boundary to Anglo Saxon cries of "Owzat… That was never out!"

Upon seeing the descending Paras, they pulled stumps and ran to their weapons and opened fire, they were so engrossed in the game they hadn't heard the command, "Action!"

Dickie said, "We'll have to cut that bit… Can't have the Germans playing cricket in the middle of the battle! Sort of gives the game away somewhat!"

I remember Dave English some time after this standing cricket bat in hand and saying, "I'm going to start a cricketing academy for disadvantaged kids and I'm going to train them and feed them into the England team!"

I looked around at us bunch of ragamuffins in the middle of a simulated bombsite in the middle of Holland and thought, *Unlikely… to say the least!*

Forty years later David has raised over £17 Million for charity, discovered and trained over seventy English international cricketers and around 700 first class cricketers through his charity cricket team Bunberry's. He has been made a Commander of the British Empire for his gallant efforts.

And the logo for his team…? A grinning rabbit with a set of jaunty ears leaning casually on a cricket bat and wearing a pair of cricket pads! All inspired, I believe, by Dave Auker wandering around with what looked like a cricket ball stuck in his hand for a couple of months.

“Norman”

A few days after poor old Dave Auker broke his hand on Norman’s doorpost, we were sent to the Amersfoort tank training ground, which had been an SS barracks during the war, to film all the second unit sequences under the instruction of Bert Batt, the second unit director.

This was basically all the action with the British tanks trying to punch through the German lines to get to Arnhem. It actually was quite dangerous as there were loads of tanks sweeping around the place, and explosives buried all around the area, which used to go off unexpectedly during the takes and we never quite knew where.

Norman and I were teamed up on a Vickers Machine Gun which was a two man job.

Norman was the number one in that he was responsible for firing the weapon; I was the number two, responsible for feeding the belt of rounds into the breech and making sure that the barrel was cooled by ensuring a plentiful water supply into the sleeve around the barrel, which was there to keep the barrel from over heating.

When you wanted to move the Vickers one would remove a locking pin under the breech, which attached it to the tripod.

The number two would lift the barrel clear and run with the ammunition and the cooling can and hose to the next position. The number one would then carry the heavy cast iron tripod, which weighed about half a hundredweight to the next position. The gun would then be reassembled rapidly and commence firing again.

It was very hot and Norman's hands were probably quite sweaty; anyway, the tripod slipped out of Norman's hands and landed on his foot, breaking it!

Poor old Norman was in agony and had to be carried from the field and placed in a safe location out of the way.

Production Pete, one of the assistant directors, inspected him and said he needed to go to the hospital.

"I know where it is," I told him, as I'd taken Dave Auker there the previous day to have the cricket ball strapped into his hand. As I had my car on location and I knew where the hospital was, it was decided that I should take Norman there and then back to the old folks' home.

A few hours later, with his foot in plaster, Norman hobbled in to the old folks' home to be met by Dave Auker who was there convalescing with his hand in plaster.

Norman looked at Dave's hand and Dave looked at Norman's foot; they then looked at each other and, both recognising the irony of the situation, gave each other a big grin and then a hug. I went off to my room for a kip as I wanted to rest in preparation for the evening's debauchery in the bars and clubs of Deventer.

The routine amongst the lads used to be finish work at about 6pm, kip till about 10pm, get up, iron your gear, shower and then hit the clubs till about 3am, sleep till 7am and then get up and go to work… no wonder we were knackered after a few months!

Sometimes I'd fall asleep at 6pm and sleep right through till

6 am and wake up feeling like I'd been reborn but furious that I'd missed a night's sport!

One night I woke up at 10pm and went to use the iron to press my gear and found that some stupid fucker had messed it up by using it to iron the pimples off his army boots! There were a couple of ex-soldiers with us who were anal about the old army bullshit!

Norman had been a war photographer and had covered the war between Nigeria and Biafra and had spent some time in a Nigerian prison as they wanted him to hand over the photo's that he'd taken... After doing *Porridge* in a Nigerian nick he decided to become an actor and went to RADA, where he played, apparently to critical acclaim, *Henry the IV, Part One*, *Henry the IV, Part Two* and *Henry V*.

Fucking hell, I thought, *The nearest I've got to the classics is playing the butler in* The Hollow *at Folkestone rep!* I'd have loved to have a crack at *Henry V*!

I never went to drama school; I was encouraged by my parents, who were both actors, not to bother. My father, who later went on to be nominated for an Emmy, said, "It took me ten years to get over my drama school training."

He then taught me how to sing, which sorted out my vocal training, and then to fence – he was a really good swordsman and he'd won the inter-drama school sword fighting championship.

He finished by saying, "Don't worry too much about posture. Just make sure your arse doesn't stick out on stage and, basically, learn your lines and don't bump into the furniture. Keep it real – always start off with 'telephone box acting' before blowing it up to fill a theatre!"

My mother, who'd won a scholarship to RADA, echoed his sentiments and said virtually the same.

"You can either do it or you can't, *daaaahling*, no one can teach you how to act. Your best bet is to go into rep' and learn your job." So that was basically my drama school training, though I would have liked to have had a crack at *Henry V*.

One night, Norman, Big Frank, James, David Auker and myself were sitting in the Pelikaan Bar having a few beers when a large English cockney 'Geez' turned up and started taking the piss out of our haircuts. It turned out he was a new addition to the crew (we learned later that he'd only recently been let out of prison and knowing someone on the film had managed to get himself a job on the unit).

We basically ignored him and he eventually gave up trying to provoke us and wandered off. Norman then decided to limp off to the Blues Bar to repair relations with his girlfriend, which had been ruptured by the 'draught excluder' incident.

We carried on in the Pelikaan when after about half an hour Norman came staggering back in with the lower half of his face spouting blood!

"That fooking c**t who was in here earlier has just fooking head-butted me!" he managed to say. "I was chatting to my girlfriend and he tried to move in on her so I told him to fook off and the bastard nutted me in the mouth!"

I leapt to my feet. "The c**t!" I said, and went off to the Blues Bar to sort him out.

The others tried to stop me, but I wasn't listening. I went in to the Blues Bar and he wasn't there; a couple of special effects boys were sitting having a drink and I went up to them.

"D'you know where that c**t who head-butted Norman is?" I asked.

Larry, one of the guys, said, "He's in the toilet."

I went towards the toilet and they stopped me and said, "I wouldn't bother, Seb… the guy will fucking kill you. Just sit at the bar and we'll sort this out."

This gave me pause so I took a seat at the bar. One of the special effects boys went into the toilet and obviously told him he should go as he opened the toilet door and marched straight out of the bar without looking to the right or left.

I left it a couple of minutes but still furious decided to follow him out onto the street.

Larry called after me: “Leave it, Seb, you’ll get hurt.”

I wasn’t listening to him but heard him say, “Ah well on your own head be it… don’t say we didn’t warn you!”

I saw the guy’s back as he was walking up the road and with the boys’ warning echoing in my mind I decided to give myself an advantage and take him by surprise.

I knew that part of town well and I saw him turn left into the main square so I decided to nip up an alleyway that came into the square further up and jump him as he walked past. I picked up a dustbin lid that I was going to use to smash in his face before attempting to leather the fuck out of him.

I waited at the end of the alleyway which joined the square… I waited and I waited and I waited and he didn’t come past. So I put down my dustbin lid and walked back down the side of the square to the Pelikaan where all the other boys were. I walked in and the place was wrecked! The boys were still there and said, “You missed it, Seebo, you fucking missed it!”

“What… what?!” I said.

Frank spoke, “The guy walked in and James called him a c**t. He turned round and said, ‘Who called me a c**t?’ and James pointed to me and said, ‘He did!’ As he turned to look at me, James caught him with a beautiful one right on the chin and then we all jumped on him and kicked the fuck out of him! He’s gone off now to get a shooter to kill us all with.”

“What a load of bollocks,” I said. “He hasn’t got a shooter!”

We decided we’d had enough for one night and decided to leave; Norman had hobbled off some time before.

As we left the Pelikaan there was the ‘geez’ on the other side of the square waiting for us. He raised a pistol, pointed it at

Big Frank, who'd done the most damage to him, and pulled the trigger!

There was a flash, a crack and a sort off *ding whirr* as the round hit the wall about three feet from Frank's head! Well, that was enough for us; we dispersed like a bunch of startled jackrabbits. There was a scream from a woman outside one of the bars and the guy disappeared.

We got back to the old folks' home, locked all the doors and kept watch. We saw blue lights flashing in the night sky as the local Dutch police did their duty and nicked him.

Norman meanwhile had taken a taxi to the hospital and returned with ten stitches in his mouth: five in the upper lip and five in the lower lip.

This rendered him speechless for a while, which in some ways was quite pleasant.

We used to catch him sniggering silently at some joke or other every now and again so as not to break open his stitches. Something tickled him one lunchtime and he started to snigger silently but uncontrollably.

I quipped, "Oh look," I said. "Norman's in stitches!" he opened his mouth wider to allow himself to laugh and all his stitches broke! Spilling a large amount of blood on to his dinner plate to the mirthful delight of the watching APA and, "YOU FOOKING BASTARD, ABINERI!" from Norman.

I had to take him back to the hospital to have his mouth stitched again… poor old Norman.

Towards the end of filming, Dickie Attenborough decided to shoot the sequence when the Paras surrendered at the end of the battle.

This is where the 1st Airborne Division, shattered, exhausted, and with no ammunition, waited for the SS to come and take them prisoner. As they sat waiting for the end, they sang the hymn 'Abide With Me'.

Dickie was busy organising the shot and telling us what was going to happen.

"Right, boys, when I say 'Action' the camera's going to start panning across you. Remember, you've all been fighting for six days without any sleep and you're all exhausted. On my hand signal, Jefferey's going to start playing 'Abide With Me' on the flute. The Germans are then going to start coming across the small bridge over there to take your surrender and that is when one by one you all start singing 'Abide with Me'... OK?"

He returned to his position behind the camera. "Right, boys... Stand by... and, Action!"

The flute started to play, the Germans started their advance across the bridge... we were all just getting ready to start singing 'Abide With Me' when Norman said loudly in his Lancashire accent, "WE'RE NOT GOING TO SURRENDER TO THAT FOOKING BUNCH OF WANKERS, ARE WE!?"

"Cut! Who said that?"

No one said a word, we kept Norman's final tribute to the 1st Airborne Division a secret.

"The Wild Colonial Boy"

Sitting on his stool in the safari club holding court was Farrell Sheridan or the Man From Mullingar as we used to call him; his father was Joe Sheridan, the Irish MP for West Meath.

I found Farrell fascinating: he had just graduated from RADA and had the persona of Marlon Brando, Richard Harris and Brendan Behan all rolled into one.

He gave the impression of very probably being a slightly misunderstood great actor (RADA has the reputation of either producing great actors or postmen, and I was sure Farrell fell in to the former category).

Wanting to be considered a great actor myself I naturally gravitated towards his orbit where I was welcomed in like a wandering fellow traveller.

I loved being in his company, he was like a mad elemental gypsy poet… meat and drink to a young aspirant like me. I learned later, though, that if he invited you for a drink that you needed to check your diary to make sure that you had at least a couple of weeks clear.

I noticed during one of our breaks in filming, where we had a few days off every now and then, that he'd disappeared; he turned up two days later having been across to Germany where he'd bought himself an old 1940s BMW 250 Motorbike.

"D'you fancy coming for a ride, *Sebaastian*?" He used to pronounce my name in full, putting a long Irish drawl on to the 'aaas' which he made sound like 'arse' as opposed to 'ass'. "Would I? Yes, please!"

He promised to take me for a trip, but wanted to wait until he'd 'sobered up a bit; I didn't mind I was prepared to wait for as long as it took.

We used to see him every now and then with his head poking out from the reeds beside the River Ijsell, fishing rod in hand with a small Dutch boy beside him who'd fallen under his spell. Farrell, no doubt, was regaling him with stories about fishing the wild salmon rivers of Ireland.

I'd also fallen under Farrell's spell, and when I was a nine-year-old boy I would have loved to have known there were grownups like him in the world.

Anyway, our short break from filming over we returned to the bangs and explosions on *The Bridge*, where in the one hundred-degree heat we were busy having enormous fun making the film.

Late one day in the midsummer heat, Dickie wanted just one more shot of a Tiger tank coming over the bridge. Dave Tomblin ordered the tank back to its first position about a half mile down the road. They wanted to get this shot before 'wrapping' as they had another four-day break in filming coming up.

The tank turned on its tracks in the road but, unlike a car, a tank reverses completely differently – it sort of swivels round backward and forwards on its tracks until it faces the direction it wants to travel in.

In the one hundred-degree heat the tarmac had started to melt, which meant the tank basically ripped up the road surface. When it set off it peeled all the tarmac off which stuck to the tracks and before it could be stopped had ripped a few hundred yards of tarmac like a piece of carpet off the road thus exposing the old cobbles underneath!

Well the local police chief went nuts! He was jumping up and down, swearing at us in Dutch and English.

"*Hoch fer domme*! You fucking stupid Engelse bastards! Look vot you have done to my fucking Weg! Ve haff commuters in der morgen… I vill get der fucking zack! You… KUNTZ!"

Dickie beckoned over the Company Accountant and had a short word in his 'shell like'. The accountant went to his car and pulled out a suitcase and walked across to the apoplectic copper.

He opened the case and handed him a huge amount of guilders all in big bundles.

The policeman couldn't believe his eyes; I thought he might arrest him for a minute for pulling off a bank heist! (he was in that sort of mood!)

The accountant patted him on the back and told him to get the whole road re-asphalted.

Two hours later he had a new road! It's amazing what a few quid can do.

Mind you, the accountant wasn't a total mug, because when the 'sparks' asked him for money for 'new bubbles', lightbulbs, more cable, more gels and then… so many thousand 'unexpected money'.

The accountant asked suspiciously, "What's this 'unexpected money'?"

The spark paused and said "Errrrrrrm… that's money we didn't expect to get!"

Anyway Farrell was delighted with the pure anarchy of the occasion and said to me, "We've got a few days off, Sebastian… Do you fancy a drink?"

I innocently said, "Yes, Farrell."

Two days and two nights later, I was still sitting with Farrell in a bar… and I was totally fucked!

I looked at the clock on the wall. "Farrell, it's five in the afternoon. We've got to get up at 6am tomorrow to go to Arnhem… I've got to get some sleep."

Farrell slurred something in reply and I staggered out into the afternoon sun, which nearly blinded me, and somehow found my way back to my little truckle, where I passed out.

The sun got me again the following morning and I dragged myself out of my bed feeling terrible. I thought I'd better check on Farrell to see if he'd got home OK. I looked in his room and there he was, thank goodness, snoring his head off and with three days' growth of beard sprouting from his chin.

I wandered across and shook him. "Farrell, I said you need to wake up. The coach will be here in a few minutes."

Nothing.

The rest of the lads had been up for around twenty minutes because I could hear them downstairs in the canteen roundly abusing Ollie and making breathtakingly insulting comments about the slop he'd served them for breakfast.

"Farrell," I said more urgently, "come on… you've got to get up! If you're late, they'll send you home!"

Still nothing. I bellowed in his ear… again, nothing. I slapped him round the face… zilch.

I dragged him out of bed and threw him on the floor… and was rewarded with a groan. This encouraged me slightly so I dragged him to the shower room and shoved him into a sitting position in the shower where I left him in his underpants and turned the shower on… cold.

I then went off for a crap and sat and waited.

Eventually I heard spluttering noises, expletives and general sounds of extreme discomfort, culminating with a loud, "WHAT THE FECK AM I DOING IN HERE!"

"Come on, Farrell, you've got to get on the coach in the next ten minutes!"

I'd just heard it arrive.

"I'm not getting on the fekking coach!" He was obviously still pissed

"Well you're going to get the sack then!"

"Naah oim fekking not cos' I'm gaaing on me Boik (Bike)"! "Farrell, you can't… it's forty miles! You'll never make it;

we'll be sending you home in a box!"

"Ah well… that's all right then," and broke into a Gaelic funeral dirge ending with, "Ahmm gaaing on me boik! I'm gaaing on me fekking boik, Sebaaaschan."

James Wardoper popped his head round the door of the shower room.

"The coach is going, boys, you'd better get on… now!"

"It's all right, James," I replied, "we're going on Farrell's boik… er, bike."

James took one look at Farrell and said, "Fuckin' Hell!" and disappeared.

I came to a decision: I could either get on the coach and leave Farrell to certain death or a 'KLM job', or I could make sure he had a chance of getting there safely by going on the bike with him.

At least with me on the back he might take a little more care and hopefully my extra weight might slow him down a bit. If he fell asleep I could always shout in his ear.

The previous weeks on the shoot and our training had obviously instilled in me the *esprit de corps* not to leave a fellow APA member in the shit… no matter how pissed.

So I stupidly said, "Right… I'm coming with you!" "Ah no, Sebaaaschan, this is moi trip!"

I dragged him into the other room and threw his kit at him. "Well it's my fucking trip now because the coach has gone and I've got to get to Arnhem so you're going to have to take me or I'll get the bloody sack!"

This got through to Farrell, who also had some *esprit de corps* left. "Oh for feck's sake… I've got to take *you* now you stupid Saxon bastard… really, Sebaaaschan, you are a fekkin' nuisance!" The irony and injustice of those remarks remain with me to this day!

We somehow got kitted up and made it downstairs to the courtyard where Farrell's beautiful German bike was waiting for him. His eyes lit up and as he kicked it in to life I noticed some coordination flowing back in to him… much to my relief.

The noise of the engine echoed around the town square, I climbed on the back and we roared through the town towards Deventer Bridge.

At that time of the morning the roads were pretty empty, thank goodness, and I think for the first mile all we passed was a horse-drawn cart loaded with hay from the harvest.

I started to relax and as we roared across the bridge over the sparkling waters of the River Ijsell, I started to really enjoy the ride until Farrell, no doubt intoxicated by so much oxygen, started weaving around the road shouting, "Oim free!… Oim free!"

"Farrell… watch it, mate!" I begged. Fortunately he listened and started to drive properly again, he really knew how to ride a bike and we danced along merrily and eventually overtook the coach with the rest of the APA on their way to Arnhem.

As we passed the coach several of our companions laughed mockingly and drew their fingers across their throats to indicate what they thought our fate was going to be… which I felt was a little unkind!

We left the coach far behind and I thought, *Great, we're going to get there before them.*

We eventually arrived on the outskirts of Arnhem and thought *Right… now where do we go?* We didn't have a clue where Ginkel Heath was.

Farrell parked the bike and knocked on the door of a small house. Eventually an old woman answered the door and staggered back in shock where the sight of a World War

Two paratrooper in full kit, wearing a tin hat with camouflage netting, seemed to drag her straight back to September 1944!

She came out with probably the only English she knew, "You fall from the sky…? You fall from the sky?" she said, pointing heavenward.

"No, love," Farrell said, "we came by boik," and pointed to it.

The old woman saw me and gasped again and disappeared into her house.

Her daughter returned who spoke English and very kindly explained where Ginkel Heath was, about ten miles away on the other side of town.

Just as she'd finished, the old woman returned again with two apples and two glasses of milk on a tray "You fall from the sky… you fall from the sky," she said in wonderment as she offered us this sustenance.

Farrell and I looked at each other and we were both quite moved; we drank the milk and put the apples in our pockets and thanked her.

As we drove off I looked back and could see her waving to us she was almost dancing as she shouted, "You fall from the sky… you fall from the sky!"

We followed the directions and eventually saw the small signs the unit had put out to direct us to the location.

The other boys had only just arrived in the coach and were getting off. Farrell stopped the bike and promptly fell asleep! His head resting on the handlebars! No matter what we did, we couldn't wake him. James Wardroper came to help.

"What are we going to do, James?" I pleaded.

James thought and came to a decision. "What we'll do is stand him up for the 'roll call' in the rear rank and then, when Jack has counted us all off, we'll hide him somewhere; he can't work in that condition, we'll have to cover for him." James had obviously seen *The Colditz Story*. So this is what we did… and it worked!

We then lay Farrell down and covered him up under a huge pile of freshly mown hay and left him there.

I then spent the whole day marching backwards and forwards in the searing heat for the next ten hours!

When the day was over, I was dead on my feet and went across to the huge pile of hay under which Farrell had spent the whole day sleeping it off!

"Farrell," I said, "we're off now." The hay stirred and Farrell emerged totally sober and as fresh as a daisy.

"Ah that was a grand sleep… are you coming for a drink, Sebaaaschen?"

I wearily shook my head and climbed on to the coach with the rest of the lads where I fell into a deep, dreamless slumber.

After having got Farrell to the location safely and saved him from a KLM Job, Farrell took it upon himself to watch my back every now and again.

One day I was lying on the ground chatting to Farrell and one of the Dutch crew, a big handy sort of chap called Jumbo.

As I was very tired I kept drifting off to sleep and waking up again, because I was in this state I'd tied the sling off my Lee Enfield rifle around my wrist so that it couldn't be taken from me whilst I was asleep.

I was nudged awake by Farrell's boot and opened my eyes to see a large, powerfully built man in his late forties crouching over me. He had a long face and pale blue eyes, framed by a pair of steel-rimmed spectacles. He kept shifting his gaze from me to Farrell and across to Jumbo, who was staring at him quite intently. Farrell was looking at him with a dark Irish stare, as if his Celtic sixth sense had warned him of some sort of danger.

The man spoke. "You like your rifle, *junger* (youngster)?"

"Not particularly," I replied, "it's tied to my wrist because if someone steals it I will lose my job and be sent home."

He nodded his head and considered my answer. I got the impression that he was coming to a decision of some sort.

Alarm bells started to ring in my own head and I felt I'd better sit upright. Colonel Waddy wandered over casually.

He now started to look between the four of us Farrell drew himself up to his full height and moved towards him in a menacing 'Richard Harris' sort of manner and said, "Do yourself a favour, mate… fuck off," and stared him down.

The man looked between the four of us for a while and decided to leave. As he went he said, "I was at this battle in '44… in the Nederlandse."

Jumbo moved towards him menacingly and started to shout at him in Dutch; the man coolly looked at us, laughed, and wandered off casually.

Jumbo turned round, spitting feathers with rage. "Fucking Nederlandse… fucking liar. He is Moffen (Dutch slang for German soldier)."

Colonel Waddy turned to Farrell, nodded to him and wandered off again.

I sometimes wonder what would have happened if Farrell had not been there. The thought still makes my scalp prickle.

Some while later, Farrell left. He'd been featured in a scene and, not being a member of the football team, had been returned home the next day on the aeroplane. He didn't say goodbye; Farrell was never a great one for emotional scenes.

I was devastated, as was Big Frank, James and several others. It was a long time before anyone was allowed to occupy his stool in the Safari Club it stayed vacant for a long time as a mark of respect.

One sunny afternoon I came out of the old folks' home for some footie practice and there was the little Dutch boy, Farrell's fishing companion, holding his fishing rod. He saw me and said, "I have come to go fishing with Farrell, can you tell him I'm here?"

"I'm afraid he's gone home," I said.

The young boy was dumbstruck "What?" he said. "We are to go fishing today!"

"I'm sorry," I said, "he went home very quickly; he couldn't even say goodbye to us."

I looked at the boy's disappointed face and said, "Look, I'll take you, if you like."

The boy looked at me and just gasped the word, "Farrell!" and tears started from his eyes. He turned round and walked sadly away, his little back heaving with grief, trailing his fishing rod behind him.

I felt tears stinging my own eyes as I thought to myself, *I know, mate… I know…*

A few years later Farrell helped both myself and my young brother in what was a real emergency for us… which I will come to anon.

The Boys from The Bridge

During the time we filmed the 1st Airborne drop into Arnhem, the place was filled with British Paras and many 'top brass' who'd come over to make sure our 'bunch of luvvies' were doing things properly.

In addition a few veterans of the battle came over as well to have a sort of re-union and to remember their pals who hadn't been able to make it. With them was the man in command of holding the Bridge all those years ago, the legendary Colonel Frost.

I really don't like to use the word hero, though undoubtedly Col' Frost was one. It always reminds me of Oddball's line in *Kelly's Heroes* where he says, "To a New Yorker like you, a hero is some kind of weird sandwich… not some nut who takes on three tigers!"

Colonel Frost had driven across from England in a small mobile home and parked it by Deventer Bridge. He politely turned down the film company's offer to put him in a luxury hotel, saying that he preferred his little caravanette as he could make himself a 'brew' in the mornings and wake in the middle of the Dutch countryside instead of waiting for unit cars to transport him around.

Anyway, he was on set rather a lot.

I remember standing next to him, chatting, looking across from the far riverbank back towards the town nearby to Deventer Bridge.

"I was furious when we got to Arnhem Bridge," he said. "Why?" I replied.

"Well, it was just like this," he said. "Acres of green fields on this side of the River Rhine. We could have dropped three battalions – 1, 2 & 3 Para – straight on to the bridge on the first day, then 10, 11 and 156th Para on the second day and the Polish Brigade on the third day – a total of around 8,500 men over three days instead of the mere 600 who managed to fight their way the eight miles from the dropping zone at Ginkel Heath. I know the reconnaissance photographs showed telegraph poles on this side of the bridge, which meant gliders wouldn't have been able to land, but we could have dropped all the paratroopers there… also we should have activated the *Landlijke Knoploegen*."

"Who were they?" I asked.

"They were the local Dutch resistance, all ex-army, who had many anti-tank weapons left over from when the Germans invaded in 1940 hidden all around Arnhem. They could have seized the bridge just before we dropped: there were around a thousand of them, all battle-hardened."

"My God, you'd have probably won the battle."

"Oh, we certainly would have done because with nearly 10,000 men on the bridge with anti-tank weapons, we would definitely have held out long enough for 30 Corps to relieve us. We nearly managed it with 600, the only reason we had to stop fighting is because the ammunition ran out."

"That means that you would have got to Berlin first before the Russians and could have managed to maybe get to Poland before them and the War would have been over by Christmas '44!" I said.

Colonel Frost looked at me and nodded sadly. "It was a cock-up," he said.

I noticed that all the veterans from the battle had the same aura of sadness around them… hardly surprising, really.

One fine morning I was sitting chatting to the makeup guy and a few of the lads when I heard a Vickers machine gun reeling off the rounds at a terrific rate.

I wondered what was going on, as there was no filming happening, and Bill the Armourer jealously guarded his .303 bulleted blanks and certainly wouldn't have allowed just anyone to profligately get through them at such a rate.

I wandered around towards the arms truck and, sitting on the ground firing the Vickers, was one of the old veterans, wearing a black eye patch and two metal claws for hands, traversing side to side with the barrel – his one eye glittering in a steely sort of way.

He finally finished off the belt of ammunition looked at me and said in a rich Geordie accent, "That's the furst time ahv fired a Vickah's since I had mah hands blown off!"

He'd been manning one of the Vickers and, having nothing else, engaged a German tank with it. Apparently, if you engage a tank with small arms it forces it to shut down all it's eye slits and close up as much as possible, as if even one round got into the tank through one of the slits it would ricochet round the interior, killing and maiming.

Obviously this vastly reduces the ability of the tank crew to see, which makes it easier for a bloke to crawl up behind it with a PIAT and shove a load of high explosive up it's Jacksie.

Unfortunately, there was no PIAT handy, so the tank commander, seeing Andrew firing the Vickers, had the time to take careful aim with his tank barrel and fire a tank round straight at him.

It was a very good shot as it hit the Vickers straight in the barrel, which sort of protected Andrew somewhat, but not from having his hands blown off and being blown back with his right eye hanging on his cheek.

Andrew lay there, bleeding profusely, and was tended to by his good mate Taffy Brace who was a medic – he'd also come out to watch the filming.

Taffy put Andrew's eye back in its socket and kept it in place with a shell dressing, he then bound his arms with a couple of tourniquets and then had to rapidly go and deal with other casualties who were coming thick and fast.

Due to the amount of casualties, poor old Taffy had run out of medical supplies long ago, therefore he had no morphine to give to Andrew, or indeed anyone. He also didn't have time to loosen the tourniquets, which you need to do every now and again to allow the blood through or gangrene sets in. Andrew couldn't do it himself, as both arms were disabled. Andrew basically lay there for about three days until the end of the battle when he was taken prisoner by the Germans, by which time gangrene had set in. The Germans then amputated his hands without anaesthetic (they'd run out of it themselves) using a guillotine. He was then put in a truck and sent to the POW camp in Amersfoort. After a couple of weeks he escaped!

"Of course we did, that's what we were trained to do," Andrew told me later – with a bloke with one leg! They got twenty miles before being recaptured. No wonder the Germans respected the Paras so much and treated them relatively well after the battle.

Colonel Waddy was also taken prisoner after the battle and he'd been badly wounded three times during it: once he was shot in the groin by a sniper, he then had a shell splinter buried in his foot and to add insult to injury, having survived all of that and whilst attempting to recuperate at the casualty clearing station in the Hartenstein Hotel, a shell exploded and brought a brick wall down on him!

Colonel Waddy told me that whilst he was in prison camp he noticed the first German attempt to form a European army.

The Germans already had a Dutch SS Division, a Norwegian one, a Belgian one and various others of different nationalities.

They'd actually managed to form a small British unit known as *Der Britisches Freikorps*, who were to form the basis of a British SS Division. This was formed of a few British traitors, malcontents and Fascists who had thrown in their lot with the Fuhrer. They went in to the POW camp to gain information, act as guards and try to recruit more members. They had to pull them out of after a couple of weeks as they were being 'bumped off' at an alarming rate by the Paras!

At one point we had a new security guy who was put in charge of the arms truck. He had a fierce Doberman Pinscher attack dog on a longish rope tethered nearby.

The new guard was as German as his dog and kept bragging about what the dog would do to you if it was ever allowed off its rope.

One day, Colonel Frost was wandering past the arms truck when this dog somehow slipped its rope – I've got a horrible feeling the security guard let him off deliberately – and launched itself towards the Colonel with its jaws slavering, obviously intending to attack him.

I fumbled with my bayonet desperately trying to put it on to my rifle as I fully intended to try and kill the animal before it did the same to Colonel Frost.

Instead of running away as most men would have done, Colonel Frost seemed to swell in size and advanced upon the snarling animal.

An element of doubt seemed to cross the dog's eyes and as Frost advanced towards it he retreated from his imposing figure, put his tail between its legs and hid behind his handler whilst quivering with fear.

I thought of Churchill's quote: "The Germans are either at

your feet or at your throat!" The same seems to apply to their dogs, but only if they meet someone like Colonel Frost.

The next day the security guard had been replaced, together with his dog.

One day Jack Mckenzie, one of our trainers, happened to mention that he was going to Arnhem the next day to try and find the grave of his uncle, who had died in the battle whilst serving with the King's Own Scottish Borderers (KOSB) who came in by glider.

He was going to look for his grave at the war cemetery at Oosterbeek in Arnhem.

I had nothing on that day so I asked if I could accompany him, and Jack was happy for me to tag along.

We took the train the next day to Arnhem, which was about a fifty-mile trip, and Jack was chatting away about his time in the Glasgow police force and then the Royal Marine Commandos. Jack had basically been brought up as an orphan by a Royal Navy charity, as both his parents had been killed in bombing raids on Glasgow.

In fact even now, at the age of seventy-four, Jack still participates in ten kilometre runs to raise money for charity. When we got to Arnhem we decided to have a beer in the small cafe outside the station.

Arnhem is very near the German border and has a slightly different topography: it is more hilly than the rest of Holland, with more high ground. It also has a different atmosphere, which seems to hang over it like a darker pall. Perhaps it is because I was aware of what happened there, but there seems to be a 'darkness' about the place which has stained the atmosphere, one is very aware that thousands of men killed each other in this small area over a very short period of time.

We got the bus to Oosterbeek cemetery and as Jack had bought the beers I offered to pay the bus fare to the cemetery.

I said to the driver, "Two to Oosterbeek Cemetery, please."

The driver looked at me and said, "Are you English?" I assented. He then said, "If you are English, you do not pay."

I sat down, feeling humbled that the behaviour of my fellow countrymen had such an effect on the next generation of the Dutch in Arnhem.

We got off at the cemetery and wandered around looking at the headstones, reading the sometimes heartrending short messages from the young soldiers' parents on the tombstones and, as the song says, the average age was nineteen.

We couldn't see Jack's uncle anywhere so we went to a small house of remembrance at the gates to the cemetery to see if there was any information in there.

As we opened the door, who should be sitting there but Colonel Waddy leafing through a register of the dead soldiers. He looked up and seemed surprised to see us.

He eventually told us that he'd dropped on the second day and had checked every one of his soldiers out of the aeroplane. he said, "When I landed there was a young officer who I'd definitely seen in the aeroplane before we jumped and somehow on the way down he just 'disappeared'. I've never found out what happened to him, which meant I couldn't tell his parents."

So there was Colonel Waddy, thirty-two years later, still trying to do his job as the young officer's CO. We wandered back out into the cemetery and continued looking for Jack's uncle. Whilst we were there we met an older Dutch couple who'd also come to pay their respects.

They had been in the Dutch Resistance during the war and after the battle, they helped to hide about 500 Paras who hadn't managed to get evacuated and were trying to evade capture by the Germans.

The local Dutch people took them into their homes and hid them for around two months right under the noses of the

Germans. The Dutch were almost starving themselves, yet shared what little they had with them. By doing so each and every one of them took an appalling risk, for the penalty for doing this was almost certainly the firing squad or at best a trip to a concentration camp. Astonishingly no one gave the evaders away, though it was common knowledge amongst many people in the town as to what was going on. Eventually the Dutch Resistance managed to liaise with the Allied Army across the Rhine and organised a night time evacuation of the 500 men.

The airborne evaders were extracted by 'Easy' Company of the 101st Airborne Division, later made famous in the HBO series *Band of Brothers*.

Easy Company had recently undertaken one of the most gallant actions of World War Two by crossing the River Waal in small boats, in daylight, under heavy German fire to try to reach the beleaguered 1st Airborne in Arnhem. They were very happy to have finished the job by rescuing 500 of their 'Airborne brothers' from under the noses of the Germans.

Sometimes I felt very humbled and also a little guilty that we were having such an amazing time on the backs of those who'd given so much at the battle, but then I thought that, were the situations reversed, the old Paras would have behaved in exactly the same way and made sure that they had as much fun as possible!

The Arnhem veterans who came over to watch the filming were very kind to us, gave us a lot of information about the battle and kept buying us beers! We felt, quite rightly, that it should be the other way around and kept buying them beers!

Then the modern-day Paras who'd filmed the drop sequences came all the way over to the Pelikaan Bar in Deventer from Arnhem to have a drink with us, and they kept buying them beers too!

Andrew Milburn, the old veteran Para with no hands and one eye, said to me, gleefully, his one eye glittering at the prospect of combat, "Huv ya been in any fights yet?"

"Just the one," I said. "When the chippies took the piss out of us... the only other fights we've had is fighting to keep Ollie's breakfasts down in the mornings."

"Ya need to huv a few fights!" he said. "We had some fooking great fights!"

"I don't fancy a fight tonight Andrew, we've got 600 Paras crammed in to the bar, we're a little bit outnumbered."

"Ahh, fooking outnumbered," he said. "We're fooking used to that! I'll tell ya what, all us old boys will come on your side!"

He was obviously warming to his theme! So I climbed out of an open window and into the relative peace and sanity of the street!

Colonel Frost used to look at the way we behaved off camera in what seemed like a strange way sometimes.

He said one day, "My goodness you remind me of my men on occasion – you behave in a very similar way when you're off duty, as it were."

"How?" I asked.

"Well, whenever you can you get as much beer down you as possible, and when you're not working, you're either asleep on the ground, smoking, drinking tea or playing football. I never believed that they could get a bunch of actors to behave so much like soldiers... Mind you," he said reflectively, "we did form the SAS from the Artists Rifles; in fact, it's still called SAS Artists Rifles."

"In your case more like APA Piss Artists Rifles," growled Bill the Armourer.

We looked at each other and nodded sagely... we were inclined to agree!

"I've got a luverly bunch of Kohkkkernuttts!"

There was a piano bar in Deventer, which had a microphone and a pianist, where we were allowed to get up and sing. There was one guy from the unit, one of the assistant directors who fancied himself as a latter-day 'crooner', and he was there all the time giving 'Misty' and 'My Way'. I don't think he went anywhere else he loved it so much!

I was in there one night with a few of the boys and he launched into *Misty* for about the seventieth time! "*Loooook at meeeee...*"

I'd had enough and shouted out, "Don't you fucking know anything else!"

He looked at me with absolute outrage and hurt with the 'ruptured bulldog' look that sometimes accompanies a heavily bruised male ego.

"No," he pouted. "Those are my two signature numbers."
"Signature numbers!" I replied. "If you sing those songs

any more, those signatures will be set in stone! And if you sing 'Misty' one more time they'll be setting up a fog alert and stop all the planes from landing at Schiphol Airport!"

The other boys in the unit started to laugh and barrack him.

That was too much for 'Bing'. Fixing me with an icy look of hauteur he carefully put the mike back in its stand and said, with as much dignity as he could summon, "You think you're so fucking good, you have a go!" He left the stage like Malvolio leaving Toby Belch where he says, "Go hang yourselves all… you are idle shallow things….I am not of your element! "

Obviously, Bing didn't think I could sing… *Wronnnng!*

I went onstage and picked up the mike. "As you like 'Misty' so much, I'm going to sing it again for you!"

He leaned back and folded his arms in a self-satisfied way, confident that a callow youth such as I would not be able to match his rendition.

What he didn't know was that I'd been taught how to sing properly, and I mean really properly. I once had a session with a pianist who was also a répétiteur at Covent Garden where I sung the duet from Act 1 V of *Otello.* I sang both parts – Iago and Otello – both tenor and baritone at the same time. The répétiteur was astonished and tried to get me to train as an opera singer, but I wanted to act.

I launched into 'Misty' and totally 'rinsed it' and sat down to thunderous applause from both the crew and Dutch alike.

I looked at Bing's shocked and downcast face and felt a bit rotten. He left the bar and shot me a pure 'Iago' look, which said, *"I'm going to get my revenge!"*… which he did eventually!

About that time there was a tragic earthquake in Italy which killed about 900 people. The local, kind-hearted Dutch set up an appeal to send relief out to the survivors.

This was publicised all over the town and sparked an idea amongst us. *Why don't we do a charity Show and get all the APA and crew on ABTF to do their 'party pieces' at the Piano Bar?*

We got there on the evening of the show and the place was full of local Dutch; the performers from the crew, though, who had promised so much talent, were conspicuous by their absence!

Apart from me, Bing, Dave English, Dave Auker and a guy who specialised in regurgitating hard-boiled eggs, there was no one else to perform, but a full house to entertain who were expected to fill a bucket with donations at the end of the evening!

We had a quick council of war. "What are we going to do?" I said.

Dave English indicated the guy who was clutching a large jar of pickled eggs.

"Put him on first whilst we have a think," Dave said.

I went over to the 'egg man' and said, "D'you mind going on first, mate?"

He said, "No, I don't mind... They usually put me on last, though, when everyone's pissed."

"Oh," I said and indicated the jar he was clutching. "Where did you get those?"

"From a bloke who runs a bar down by the river," he said. "I'll give them back to him after the show."

"But they'll have been down in your gut!" I said

"They're not going to stay there," he said. "I'll bring 'em back up, put them back in the jar and take them back to him!"

I went green, nodded and went back to our table. "He'll go on first," I said.

"Great," said Dave, and jumped on the stage to introduce the show.

Dave was a real showman and quickly got the audience on our side. He then indicated to the pianist to play the introduction whilst the 'egg man' got himself prepared.

The 'egg man' came on with his jar of pickled eggs and said, "Oh my goodness, I'm really hungry... it's lucky I found these by the side of the road!" he then unscrewed the jar and swallowed about twenty pickled eggs whole one at a time!

The audience looked on in bemused silence and offered no

reaction at all apart from one of the APA who was watching an actor called Patrick Hannaway who started to emit a high pitched scream of laughter.

The 'egg man' rubbed his tummy in discomfort and said, "Oh dear I think they're a bit off!"

He then held the open jar in front of him and proceeded with unerring accuracy to project the twenty eggs with great speed back into the jar!

Several of the audience made gagging noises and one or two went *eeeeugh*!

Patrick Hannaway, however, leapt to his feet and gave him a standing ovation whilst screaming with hysterical laughter!

Bing went on and sang 'Misty', which went down well and he left the stage with an 'I told you so!' look in my direction.

Dave English did about ten minutes of telling jokes, which went down well with the English crew.

Dave Auker, billed as 'Dainty Dave' (he was built like a bull), gave a really nice camp tap dancing routine which went down very well with everyone.

I then went on and sang some Schubert Lieder 'Der Tod und das Madchen', which didn't go down that well with the English, but much better with the more cultured Dutch who also understood the words better. All in all not a total disaster!

Dave English decided that we needed a finale. "What are we going to do?" I asked

"We'll do 'I've got a luverly bunch of coconuts'," Dave said. "I don't know the words," I replied.

"Don't worry, Seebo, just follow us."

Dave Auker, Bing, Dave English and myself took to the stage for the finale.

The 'egg man' didn't join us; he was busy rowing with his Dutch girlfriend who was trying to terminate their relationship.

We launched into the finale, of course, the Dutch had never heard 'I've got a luverly bunch of coconuts' and it was awful.

I didn't know the words and was busy mouthing them like John Redwood trying to sing the Welsh National Anthem; the two Dave's eventually ran out of words and started to invent their own obscene version. The Dutch stared at us blankly whilst Patrick Hannaway started to scream and scream and scream with laughter.

Eventually he started to make a sort of '*herrrrgg*' noise mixed with his screams of mirth, we'd hear a scream, *herrrgg*, scream, *herrrgg*, scream, *herrrg*, and then a *crash* as he collapsed across a couple of tables bringing bottles and glasses down with him. He started to crawl out of the bar, making the same noise. Eventually he got outside and we could hear muffled screams mixed with *herrrgs* as we carried on singing 'I've got a luverly bunch of coconuts!'

Blue lights started to converge on the square and we were aware of Patrick being loaded into an ambulance to the sounds of *scream....herrrrgg*.

We enquired of his health to the hospital after the show.

They said that he was laughing so much that his lung had collapsed and that despite the pain, hysteria had taken such a hold that he couldn't stop screaming with laughter!

He'd crawled out of the club to get away from our singing but to no avail, as there was a loudspeaker outside the club still relaying 'I've got a luverly bunch of coconuts!'

"He nearly died," said the doctor. "And no, you can't come and visit as we don't want him to start laughing again!"

Pity! We were going to take him a bunch of coconuts as a get well present!

"Nanny!"

Jack Dearlove, 'Jacko' as we called him, was our chaperone, mentor and moral guardian whilst in Holland.

He was an ex-Desert Rat and was in a 'recce' squadron in the 8th Army during the war.

Recce is a very dangerous job. Your task is to stay in contact with the enemy at all times and report back to the main force on their dispositions. Basically, the job is to shadow the enemy without them seeing you, in a small armoured vehicle called a Bren Gun Carrier, which is designed to get you out of trouble really quickly if detected.

I think the stress of doing this for a few years told on Jacko, to the extent that he used to worry about everything. He used to get us up in the mornings, not an easy task after we'd been on the town the night before, with shouts of, "Come on, my beauties!... Stop playing with yourselves! Hands off cocks, feet in socks! Geeeeet up, yew lazy baaaastards!"

There was one actor in particular who really used to resent Jacko's morning exhortations and used to deliberately exasperate him by lying in bed until the last minute.

He pretended to be asleep one morning and Jacko shook him by the shoulder. The actor made an unexpected violent lunge towards him saying, "I told you never to touch me in the mornings, you 'orribble little rat. Touch me again and I'll break your fucking neck!"

Jacko recoiled from him in terror and never went near him again; he still used to wake him, though, by prodding him with a twenty-foot pole from a safe distance! Whilst the actor used to lie in bed glaring and hurling obscenities at him!

Jacko responded with, "Wouldn't have done it in my day, son. We'd have you straight down the fucking glasshouse! Then, we'd take you behind a four-tonne truck and kick the shite out of you!"

That was basically our morning routine: we'd wake up by being abused by Jacko – no doubt after some of the APA had been abusing themselves half the night! – then we'd go downstairs and we'd *all* abuse Ollie for the shit breakfast he'd served up.

Basically the start to our day was a cycle of abuse… I'm sure a psychiatrist would have had a field day! Jacko's job was to make sure we were available to go on set whenever we were required. Sometimes, though, we didn't want to go on set as it involved being 'featured' if we were placed too close to the camera. This meant that you were then given a KLM job and sent home. Even the guys in the football team who were supposed to be immune to this fate still didn't want to chance it.

So a small team of us – basically myself, James, Norman, Big Frank, Dave Auker and Dave English – used to try and hide from Jacko when we were on set.

If Dave Tomblin said to Jacko, "Get me three APA as we want to dress them in the shot," we'd try and make sure we weren't around, hoping that Jacko would grab the three nearest to hand and take them to run the risk of being sent home. If we were nabbed by Jacko we would put a bandage across our face or wear a helmet that was too big, anything to avoid being seen clearly by the camera.

We developed a strategy, which we kept strictly to ourselves, where we'd kill two birds with one stone. We'd avoid Jacko and get some much needed kip at the same time in order to prepare ourselves physically for the evening ahead.

We secreted a large camouflage net which was used to hide a field gun and keep it near us on set and when opportunity presented itself and Jacko wasn't around we'd find a ditch or a piece of open ground, cover ourselves in the netting, put foliage on top and have a few hours 'snuzzle' as Norman used to call it. This worked well for a long time and often we'd hear Jacko passing close by saying "Where have those bastards got to?"

Jacko was also mad keen on football and was an avid supporter of the Hammers.

He appointed himself coach of our football team and was always there when we were practising. Jacko decided to give me some specialist goalkeeping training.

"The trouble with you, Seebo," he used to say, "is you're just like Mervyn Day (the then West Ham goalie). He's a short arse, just like you and he comes off his goal line too often… just like you! You've got to time coming off your goal line properly and you've got to time your jumps for the high crosses."

He then took me to some goalposts on the other side of the river with a couple of the guys and then made me practice grabbing high crosses and timing my forays off the goal line. I must say, it actually improved my goalkeeping performances markedly!

One day we were having our afternoon 'snuzzle' under our camouflage net and awoke in the late afternoon to find ourselves surrounded by Sherman tanks! Some of them were quite close… we were so well camouflaged that they couldn't see us! We were really close to getting crushed under their tracks!

We never pulled that trick again – unless we were near woods, then we'd kip in there as the tanks couldn't get in there. I told Jacko this story towards the end of filming when I thought it didn't matter anymore and he went pale.

"That reminds me of when we landed in Italy in1943," he told me. "We were parked just off the beach on a piece of grass in front of our whole regiment, waiting for the order to move off after the retreating Germans. After a few days we got the order to move and followed them as far as Rome. We were really looking forward to liberating Rome, as we could have a few beers, spag' boll and vino. We'd been living on bully beef for the last few weeks. Anyway, we got in to Rome and Jerrie had fucked off so we had the place to ourselves. We had plenty of money as we'd had nothing to spend it on for ages, so we found a bar and made ourselves comfortable. A few hours later the rest of our regiment turned up, saw our Bren Gun Carrier parked outside and came in to the bar and as soon as they saw us they said…

"Fucking hell, you lucky bastards!"

"What are you talking about?" asked Jacko.

"Well, you know when you moved off the beach? We were all watching you… you drove round the corner and left a patch of yellow grass where the Bren Gun Carrier had been for the last four days… two minutes after you'd gone this fucking great German .88 shell landed right in the middle of that patch of grass… we fucking pissed ourselves! You lucky bastards!"

Jacko said, "I nearly passed out at the thought." Poor old Jacko! No wonder he was so nervous!

"A Very, Very Bad Day!"

It started off well.

It was a lovely fine day and we were filming a sequence at Frost's house, the main location at the bridge.

Frost's house had been constructed of wood and plastic bricks, and the interiors were decked out with period furnishings and props for interior sequences.

The scene we were filming was some time in to the battle, so there was a fair amount of rubble from the battle and flames coming out of the roof of the house generated by little flame-throwing devices attached to large Calor gas cylinders in the roof of the house. Watching the realistic proceedings was a large crowd of at least 500 local people.

Then it happened: one of the little flame-throwers set light to part of the roof. The head of special effects went in calmly on the ground floor to rescue the period furniture and I followed to give him a hand.

We were making reasonable progress, but I still turned to him and said, "This would go a lot quicker if some of the others gave us a hand."

"Oh, they won't come in here," he said. "Why not?" I asked.

"Because they know that there are ten big Calor gas

cylinders in the roof and that, if they go off, there'll be a fucking great explosion with shrapnel from the cylinders flying all over the town. Hang on a minute, I'd forgotten about those!" and with that he rushed off upstairs!

Well, I lost it, and immediately became like Corporal Jones from *Dad's Army* – "Don't panic, don't panic!"

I bravely ran out of the house shouting, "The whole thing's going to explode! There's a load of gas cylinders in the roof! The whole place is like a fucking great bomb! Take cover! Save yourselves! Save yourselves! We're all going to fucking die!"

Nobody seemed to be taking any notice! So I rushed across to the barrier standing behind which were about 500 Dutch spectators.

I waved my arms at them.

"Go," I said. "Run! there's going to be a big bang… run!"

They just stood there, smiling amiably at me and nodding but not moving.

Oh fuck it! I thought, and dived behind a small stone wall, clasped my helmet to the top of my head and whimpered whilst waiting for Armageddon – I was allowed to behave like a coward in front of the Dutch on this day as I was dressed as a German soldier, not a British Para!

Nothing happened!

I ventured a peek over the top of the wall and saw the head of special effects staggering out of the house with a dirty great gas cylinder on his shoulder; he'd already retrieved about half a dozen of them and brought them to safety. It was actually one of the bravest things I'd ever seen, because the last few cylinders he rescued literally blistered his hands – they were ready to explode.

I went up and apologised to him for abandoning him. "That's all right, Seb," he replied. "At least you came in with me… no other fucker did."

"Yeah, but I didn't know… Oh well!"

There was an assistant director on the film whose name was Jerry; he was the son of a famous Hollywood family.

The assistant director's job on a movie isn't as nearly as grand as it sounds. It basically involves making sure the relevant actors are on set when needed, running around performing errands and carrying out traffic and crowd control duties.

Jerry, naturally, was aching to do something a little more 'creative'.

Well, he got his opportunity.

Dickie Attenborough wanted a 'pick up' shot, which he didn't have time to do himself, of some riflemen firing behind sandbags, a Bren Gun chattering away and finally a PIAT firing, when they would then cut to a tank exploding, but they already had that shot.

A PIAT (Personal Infantry Anti Tank Weapon) is like a heavy crossbow which catapults a large finned anti tank projectile used for destroying – yes, you guessed it – tanks!

The main unit with Dickie and Dave Tomblin were moving to another location, so Dave Tomblin left behind a camera operator, Jerry, Bill the Armourer and a few of us APA to make this little sequence.

Before he went he had a very serious word with Jerry. "Now, Jerry, we want you to film these three sequences, but on no account are you to put the camera any where near the weapons! We don't care what happens to you, the APA or Bill the Armourer, but *if anything* happens to that bloody camera I will actually string you up by your little toes! Do you understand me?!"

"Oh yeah, Dave, cool man!" he said in his laid-back Californian style.

Dave Tomblin didn't look reassured. "I mean it, Jerry… nothing must happen to that camera, if it does, I'll kill you! And worse than that, it'll be the end of your career!"

Everybody knows that breaking a camera on a film shoot is a capital offence. Dave and the rest of the main unit went off and Jerry settled down to film the 'pick ups'.

It all went fine, we banged away with our Lee Enfields and David Killick, who used to call his Bren Gun 'Slack Alice', performed his duties in an exemplary manner.

Then it was time to fire the PIAT.

Flushed with success, Jerry decided to get a little ambitious with the PIAT.

"What would make a great shot is if you had the PIAT shell going straight towards the camera as the tank driver's POV (point of view)!" said Jerry.

I inwardly groaned. *Oh no*, I thought, *he's actually going to try and do it!*

"Er, how are you going to do that with out hitting the camera, Jerry?" someone asked.

"I've got a sheet of unbreakable glass which we can put in front of the camera and the camera can film the PIAT shell flying towards it and then it will bounce off without touching the camera, and we'll get a great shot!"

Christ! I thought, but didn't say anything, the director is the director and it doesn't do to question him too often… even a greenhorn like Jerry.

They set the shot up, Bill the Armourer made himself comfortable with the PIAT behind a pile of sandbags, the cameraman took up position behind the sheet of unbreakable glass, and Jerry said, "Turn over! PIAT sequence take 1, aaaaand *action*!"

Bill fired the PIAT shell, which went straight through the 'unbreakable' glass, through all the lenses in the camera and rested in the main body of the camera with its fins poking out. The poor cameramen gave a cry of pain and fell backwards clutching his eye, which had been right up against the eyepiece and taken the full impact!

Bill the Armourer said to the cameraman, "You're the only tank commander who'se seen that and lived!"

Jerry made himself scarce rapidly!

We were left with a cameraman with an eye like a ripe plum and a camera with a PIAT shell poking out of it. Word got to Dave Tomblin and he came haring back to see for himself. He surveyed what had happened and the broken camera and went various different colours with rage.

"Where is he!" he said with a sort of quiet menace. "WHERE IS HE!" he bellowed and shot off looking for him.

Jerry had made himself extremely scarce and when David found him, he'd calmed down considerably, but he still received an enormous rocket up his arse! Almost as big as the PIAT!

We broke for lunch at which we had plenty to discuss.

Dave Tomblin and Dickie were busy trying to put the morning's disasters behind them and focus on the next sequence which involved a Tiger Tank coming round the corner of Frost's house – which had nearly caught fire that morning – followed by German infantry who were to engage the British in close quarters combat.

The local Dutch army unit had lent us a modern Leopard Tank which the design department had made to look like a World War Two Tiger. The tank and its Dutch crew arrived with a squeak, clank and a roar of exhaust.

The tank commander opened the hatch and was wreathed in smoke from the inside; you could tell by the sweet musky smell that it wasn't diesel exhaust… they'd been sitting in there smoking their Dutch wacky baccy!

They'd also been drinking, as a crew member popped up from the interior with a bottle of Martini and a half bottle of Vodka. He proceeded to mix the two beverages together and made themselves a couple of large vodka martini's whilst they shared the joint!

All the crew had very long hair and beards, which they'd

tucked into hairnets. They'd split the APA into two groups, one to portray German SS and the other group the Paras.

We looked at each other and thought, *We really don't fancy working with this bunch of jokers driving a lethal tank around when they're high as kites and totally arseholed!*

I was in the German group, which was supposed to follow the tank down the side of Frost's house and into the main road where we were supposed to open up with automatic fire at the windows before being jumped and bayonetted by the Paras (we were using real bayonets!)

Blimey! I thought, *There's so much that could go wrong in this sequence.*

I started, not for the first time that day, to feel a bit anxious.

Dave Tomblin took up position behind the camera and shouted into his loudhailer.

"We're not going to rehearse this sequence… we're going to go straight for it. When I say 'action', I want the tank to come down the side of the house and turn left into the main street, the APA will follow and fire into the windows. When the tank reaches the lamp-post, the Paras will come out and engage the German APA and then we'll cut. RIGHT, STAND BY EVERYONE. GOING FOR A TAKE. SOUND RUNNING, ROLLING, AND… ACTION!"

The tank lurched forwards, but instead of going past the house it bulldozed straight through it, thereby completely demolishing the house the special effects guy had risked his life to preserve earlier that day.

The unit went ballistic. "CUT… CUT… CUT… !" shouted Dave. "Stop that fucking tank, for fuck's sake!"

The tank squealed to a halt like an errant steam engine. "Fucking hell," shouted Dave (that was the only time he'd ever sworn on set.)

Poor Dickie burst into floods of tears.

We still had six weeks of interior scenes scheduled in that

building; it was lucky that myself and the special effects guy had got so much of the furniture and dressings out earlier otherwise they'd have had a real continuity problem when dressing another of the rooms which could possibly have been insurmountable.

"OK, that's a wrap," David said wearily and we all dispersed quietly without the customary jokey behaviour.

I heard that later that evening the boys were having their customary drink in the Pelikaan when Dave Tomblin walked in he said to them, "I want you to stop drinking now, boys, 'cos I'm going to get totally hammered and I want you to make sure I get back to my hotel."

The boys put their drinks down and proceeded to watch over David like a bunch of guardian angels as he got totally wrecked. Once he'd slumped against the bar, the boys picked him up, loaded him into a taxi, carried him to his room, took his shoes and socks off, and put him to bed.

The next day David carried on as if nothing had happened.

What a total professional; we will never see his like again.

"The Stunt Boys"

The small team of British stuntmen we had on the film were and are iconic characters in the British Film Industry.

They were Dougie Robinson, a big amiable South African; Alf Joint who was the stunt arranger, Paul Weston who was Superman's body double and also Roger Moore's stunt double in all the Bond Movies and Vic Armstrong who went on to become one of Hollywood's leading stunt arrangers. The stunt boys were on quite a nice deal, which was £500 per week guaranteed and

£50 per stunt. In today's money that's £3,500 guaranteed per week, plus £350 per stunt.

The Dutch stuntmen, however, were on a lot more than that – I think they had a better trade union – but they weren't a patch on our boys! Some of the stunts our boys did weren't that dangerous at all, but some were really dodgy! Nevertheless, they still got £50 a stunt, no matter how dangerous.

They'd just brought in a new 'airbag' for high falls from buildings, which was used to cushion stuntmen falling from height.

There was a bit of humming and hawing over this new piece of kit, as it had not really been 'used in anger' before. The stunt guys were used to falling on to cardboard boxes which had been constructed in the same way as a brick wall, with 'headers' and 'stretchers' so they can be locked together and would collapse safely under the falling stuntmans' weight.

The cardboard box method had been used since the birth of the film industry – the stuntmen were used to it and were not too happy about this new 'airbag'; however, someone had wanted to try it out and I think Alf Joint, who was head of stunts, was doing someone a favour by giving the airbag its debut. Obviously Alf felt he had to be the first one to use it as he was not the sort of man who would ask a stuntman to perform a stunt which he wasn't prepared to do himself.

I remember standing behind Alf, representing a fellow rifleman whilst Alf had to be 'shot' and then fall from the open window on to the airbag.

'Action' was called and Alf started to fire his rifle. He then had to be shot; a blood capsule exploded on his chest, he dropped his rifle, clutched his chest and dropped out of my vision towards the airbag.

He landed and everyone went quiet. Dickie Attenborough said, "Cut" and I could hear, "Is he all right?" and "Get the medic here now!"

Apparently the airbag hadn't been inflated enough and had only partially broken Alf 's fall which had not stopped him from breaking his collarbone; it could have been a lot worse.

I believe the airbag was parked for a few years after that, but is now used on movies all the time.

One of the stuntmen was a lovely man with a heart of gold and the courage of a lion, but he made a bit of a 'tit' of himself on one stunt.

He was portraying a big tough SS man and he had to approach a doorway to a building occupied by Paras, hurl a grenade in and after it exploded rake the room with machine gun fire and then go in.

What he did was sling in the German stick grenade and, without waiting for it to explode, followed it in!

We all started shouting, "No! No! Stop! Come out, you stupid bugger!"

Then the inevitable happened there was a loud *bang*, a horrible pause and then he staggered out pitch black from head to toe and with his uniform on fire! But, apart from that, completely unharmed.

Colonel Waddy stood shaking his head from side to side and saying, "No, no, no, that's not how it's done!"

Paul Weston was relaxing in his caravan one morning when an AD came in and told him that, "We need a stunt double for Ryan O'Neal tomorrow. We've asked the Dutch guys to do it but they say it's too dangerous, so you're going to have to!"

Paul thought, *Here we go!*

"What does it involve?" he asked.

The AD said, "General Gavin, who O'Neal is playing, had a heavy landing when he jumped in 1944 and broke his back. He kept quiet and carried on with his duties We need someone to stand in for 'O Neal as he parachutes in and hits the ground. It's too difficult to do it with a normal parachute as we need to have quite a 'tight' shot; obviously we're going to cut when you hit the ground, and then O'Neal will replace you and then limp off."

In order to get this 'tight' shot they weren't going to have the stunt guy come down on a normal parachute. What they'd done was create a special 'rig' where the parachute was pinned open on a large circular steel frame held securely by pins which could be removed by pressing a lever.

The opened parachute and the stuntman would then be lifted up on the rig by crane and was expected to remain suspended there until the aircraft were in vision at the back of the shot and started to drop the parachutists. With the dropping Paras in the background they would then release the pins on the stuntman's parachute, who was to float down in the foreground until he landed. At this point Ryan O'Neal would be placed in the harness after the drop.

Paul asked, "Has this ever been done before?" "Er, no," said the AD.

The AD said, "All the Dutch stuntmen have refused to do this, Vic Armstrong can't do it as he doesn't look enough like Ryan 'O Neal, Alf Joint's broken his collarbone and nobody else does falls from height."

Paul obviously looked extremely doubtful as the AD said, "Look, I know it's dodgy, mate, but we need this shot and if you do this we'll owe you one."

Paul said, "For fifty quid!"

The AD said, "Oh yes, for fifty quid, mate!"

Paul was at the beginning of his career and knew that if you 'bottled' a stunt that word would get around; on the other hand, he didn't fancy being a guinea pig on an untried piece of kit which would drop him to the earth from about seventy-five foot in the air. He'd seen what had happened with the 'airbag'.

Being a young man with an enormous amount of pride and, it goes without saying, a huge degree of courage, he agreed to do it.

A relieved AD patted him on the back and said, "Thanks, mate. As I say, we owe you one!"

Paul then spent a restless night thinking about what could go wrong.

The next day we all turned up on set. There were about 500 Dutch extra's on the ground, us APA at the foreground of the shot, arriving by air were around 100 British Paras, only this time dressed as American troops, and there was Paul surveying this Heath Robinson contraption that was to haul him in to the air.

I was chatting to him as he was getting into his harness and attached to the rig. I said, "How are you feeling, mate?"

"Oh, not too bad, Seebo," he said coolly. "Little bit worried about this wind, though."

I hadn't noticed but it was beginning to pick up somewhat.

Dave Tomblin shouted into the loudhailer, "Get that rig into the air!"

The crane driver extended the arm of his crane and hoisted Paul into the air where he dangled helplessly; the only things keeping him safe were the few metal pins attaching the opened parachute to the steel frame.

I chatted to him from the ground trying to keep his spirits up whilst he hung there waiting to be dropped. His rig was beginning to swing and creak in the wind in rather an unnerving way.

Quietly I was thinking that, *I hope his legs don't go numb*, as he'd been hanging there for about twenty minutes and all the blood must have rushed to his feet.

Finally, we heard from the unit, "Stand by! Aircraft are in the air!" The planes flew overhead and started to eject the paratroopers.

"And action, Paul."

They pulled the pins out of Paul's parachute and he hurtled towards the ground. Even though the 'chute was open it still takes time to inflate with air before it can start to arrest your fall.

In this case the 'chute didn't inflate until it was about fifteen feet up which meant that Paul hit the ground at a hell of a speed.

I rushed across once they'd said 'cut' to see how he was. Thankfully he seemed to be OK: he hadn't broken anything and seemed to be moving around alright.

"I didn't land properly because I couldn't feel my legs," Paul said.

I knew it! I thought.

"Well you've done it now. Well done, mate, they wont ask

you to do that again." You only ever do that dangerous a stunt once. If the cameras don't catch it, tough!"

At which point Dave Tomblin said, "First positions as soon as you can, we're going again!"

I couldn't believe it.

An ashen-faced Paul was getting back into his rig as he prepared to go through the ordeal again.

"Are you going to be OK, mate?" I asked

"Yeah, I'll be fine, Seebo. I've done it once and lived, I guess I will again."

They hauled him up and prepared to repeat the whole dangerous exercise once more.

The planes were in the air, only this time the wind had really 'got up' and Paul's rig was swinging wildly.

The unit said 'stand by'.

Paul shouted down to me, "Seebo my parachute's coming away!"

I looked up and saw that half of Paul's parachute had come unpinned from the rig and was flapping uselessly in the breeze.

If he came down with just half a parachute it would have no chance of inflating at all and Paul could die!

I rushed across to the unit, who were gazing skyward at the approaching aircraft, and said, "Paul's parachute's coming undone. You'll have to bring him down!"

They either didn't hear me or they ignored me. I then rushed across to the crane driver and said, "Lower the crane – bring him down!"

I was really risking a KLM job by behaving like this… football team or not! The crane driver definitely ignored me.

The Paras dropped and the call came: "ACTION, PAUL!"

They unpinned the rest of Paul's 'chute and he came hurtling down at a horrendous speed; his parachute had inflated a little but he still hit the ground really hard and I heard a horrible 'crack' as his leg broke.

I rushed up to Paul who was writhing in pain. He looked at me and said, "Thanks for trying to save my arse, Seebo! At least I get to have some time off now!"

The ambulance arrived and carted him off to hospital, I offered to take him in my car like I had everyone else, but Paul said he fancied a few painkillers!

Dave Tomblin really appreciated what Paul had done and that one act of courage and dedication to his craft basically made Paul's career and he worked on so many movies after that: *Superman*, Bond films and all the Indiana Jones movies… and quite right too!

What was fantastic was that Paul was now *hors de combat*, what with being injured. It meant that he was able to join us APA in the evenings and we had a wonderful time with him whilst he hobbled about the dance floors of Deventer, no longer having to get to bed early just in case he was called on in the morning to risk life and limb.

He was a very welcome addition to our revels!

"Crossing The Waal"

We were approaching the end of the shoot and began to sense that bitter sweet feeling one used to get as a kid as we approached the end of the summer holidays: a feeling of sadness mixed with 'lets make the most of each day left'.

I'm beginning to get a similar feeling now I'm in my sixty-third year!

Jacko' got us up one morning with his customary "Get up, you lazy baaastards! Hands off cocks, feet in socks!"

We opened our bleary eyes and saw him doling out inflatable lifejackets to the end of each bed.

"Right, put your American gear on this morning and put these lifejackets on underneath."

We asked Jacko what was going on.

"I dunno," he said. "I've just been told you've all got to wear them, so you'd better put them on... No time for breakfast today, boys, they'll give you some from the catering wagons when we reach the location."

I caught the two boys from 1 Para looking at the lifejackets in a doubtful way. We boarded the coach and wondered where we were off to.

It was quite a long drive: we drove through Arnhem, which

was about forty miles over Arnhem Bridge and onward through the Dutch countryside eventually we drove past a sign that said Nijmegen and approached a large twin spanned steel Bridge, even bigger than Arnhem Bridge.

The whole area was a hive of activity; it looked like the entire German Army had just 'popped over' to Holland for a quick visit! There were rows of tanks, hundreds of men dressed in German uniform and Dutch police letting traffic in from Germany over Nijmegen Bridge.

The occupants of the cars coming in to Holland from Germany gazed out of their windows in astonishment at the sight. There was a roar of anger from the Dutch extras who all charged at one particular car and had to be prevented by the Dutch police from picking it up and slinging it into the river. Apparently one German guy, upon seeing the 9th and 10th Frundsberg and Hohenstaufen Divisions on the bridge, had stuck his right arm out of the car window in a saluting gesture a la 'Sieg Heil' and delivered a German peroration of approval.

A Dutch extra in full German SS uniform said to me in fury, "Fucking Germans… they never fucking learn!"

We were told to move down to the riverbank and grab some breakfast from the catering van down there and wait for instructions.

We looked at the broad expanse of the River Waal and it began to dawn on us why we'd been told to put lifejackets on under our uniforms.

Jacko wandered past saying, "If you end up in the drink, just pull the little plastic ring at the top of the lifejacket, which should hopefully inflate and then yell like fuck… there are safety boats and divers in the river who'll come and pick you up, so you'll be OK, boys!"

I thought, *KLM job or not, the first thing I'm going to do if I end up in that river is get rid of my rifle, helmet and pack, let it all sink to the bottom, and just pray that my lifejacket inflates.*

The river was broad and with a strong current moving towards the nearby Dutch coast. Some boys had made sure their lifejackets worked by inflating them under their uniform jackets, which made them look like little tubbies.

I didn't want to do that; I was prepared to take a chance and I was a good swimmer. I grabbed a cup of tea and a bacon roll and sat on the grass chatting to the two boys from 1 Para. An old British Army truck wended its way towards us with an odd-looking cargo on the trailer.

The truck stopped and a couple of guys slung the contents of the trucks on to the ground with a crash. We went up and inspected what they'd delivered. It was a pile of old World War Two collapsible boats. We pulled them to one side and tried to work out how to put them together.

Eventually we worked out how to do it. We pulled the canvas sides upwards which were attached to a wooden frame and then put struts downwards which kept the sides of the boats rigid and braced, in each boat were four sets of wooden paddles… quite easy really.

I asked the two Paras, "Are you coming in our boat?"

They looked at the vintage WW2 boat, which actually were covered in cobwebs, looked across at the other side of the river, looked at each other and then said, "Nah… it looks a bit dodgy to me."

"Dodgy?" I said. "You're a Para… one of Her Majesty's finest… dodgy!"

"I know we are," he replied. "It's just that we leave that sort of job to the Marines."

They continued to eat their bacon rolls and watched as we dragged the boats into the water.

Production Pete told us what we were going to do which was basically replicate one of the most gallant and courageous actions of World War Two, where elements of the American Airborne paddled in broad daylight under heavy fire from fixed German positions, sited in depth on the other side of the river.

They then landed, stormed those heavily defended positions and then swept to the left and secured the end of Nijmegen Bridge, thereby allowing the tanks from 30 Corps to continue their charge towards Arnhem. They lost about half their men involved in the action.

The Americans succeeded in all of their objectives and a couple of tanks from the Guards Armoured Division managed to get across, but instead of charging towards Arnhem they stopped and had a cup of tea.

This is while the British Paras were hanging on to Arnhem Bridge by their fingertips! The American officer who'd led the river crossing, asked them what the hell they thought they were playing at.

"Oh," they said. "There's a German .88 just round the corner and it might knock us out. Anyway we've been up all night!"

The Americans couldn't believe it and offered to act as infantry for them and take out the .88, but they said, "No, we're waiting here for orders!"

An enormous heroic effort had been made to take Nijmegen bridge.

The Guards were put in the position where they were within striking distance of Arnhem and they stopped. No wonder the Paras fight them every time they see them.

One of the regular Paras told me later that one of their sister battalions was on open arrest in Berlin for having broken in to the Guards' officers' mess and stolen all their regimental silver and wouldn't give it back!

Anyway, the APA started to drag the boats into the shallows and prepared themselves for their voyage across the Waal.

Each boat had a small outboard motor in, except ours! It was taken out to replace the faulty engine in Robert Redford's boat.

He was playing Colonel Sink, the leader of the gallant band who crossed the river in '44.

There were around eight guys in our boat and four paddles, which meant that we used our rifle butts as propulsion; we were doing it the way they did it in 1944.

We moved out into the river and nosed into the current, which was steady but not too strong, and we were able to head at a reasonable speed in the direction we wanted to go in without too much exertion.

We heard a sort of *pop pop* overhead as smoke canisters were fired into the air to create a smoke screen to shroud our movements from the 'Germans' on the other bank. The 'Germans' were behind a dyke on the other side of the river, which they were using as cover whilst preparing to rake us with rifle and machine gun fire.

We carried on towards them and then started to hear small arms fire and see muzzle flashes from the MG42s and Mausers on the opposite bank.

And then it happened – *Whumpa*! – a massive explosion right in the middle of our little flotilla which sent one boat and its occupants into the Waal! Then another… and another… *Whumpa*!

By this time two or three boats had gone over and the divers and safety boats were pulling the APA out of the water.

Fuck me! I thought. We all started to paddle furiously and we achieved an almost *Tom & Jerry*-like speed as we even started to overtake the boats that had engines!

In no time at all we'd reached the other bank; I picked up the rope and jumped over the side to pull the boat into the shore. In my desperation to reach dry land I'd misjudged the depth of the river and went down about seven feet before my feet hit the bottom of the river!

The weight of my pack, rifle, helmet and boots kept my feet on the riverbed and I was able to scramble along whilst holding my breath until my head broke the surface and I managed to pull the boat to the bank.

I then tried to run towards the dyke, but could hardly move because of the weight of my soaking uniform so I took cover behind a dune and banged off a few 'blanks' until they said cut. They then said, "First positions, please", and we all had to paddle back across the Waal and then do the whole thing again!

At the end of the day, after the second trip, my nerves were in a shredded state and my eyes were protruding from my head like a pair of dog's balls!

One of the Paras said to me afterwards, "Told you it was dodgy, didn't I!"

"End of Shoot Party and Journey Home"

At last the dreaded day came and they used their final piece of celluloid on *A Bridge Too Far.*

For weeks we'd been planning the 'APA Wrap Party', which was to take place at the old folks' home: for a while we'd been collecting underwear from our Dutch 'conquests', which we displayed on the wall as trophies – someone displayed an old whalebone corset, which was credited to Jacko Dearlove – and to complete the whole effect, Dave Auker had somehow worked out a way of making the vacuum cleaner blow instead of suck and tied a load of paper streamers on the end to give a wavy effect of paper streamers!

We had a record player and a load of LPs, tables loaded with sandwiches and beer and a small stage made from a few rostra, which placed by an open window at the end of the room. We'd obviously invited the whole unit and, one by one, they drifted in. Dickie Attenborough viewed the ambience in a slightly dubious manner and gradually the room filled up with Colonel Waddy and his wife, all the stunt boys, crew with wives and girlfriends, and Bing' – *Oh no*, I thought, *not "Looook at Meeeee" again!*

The party was going with a swing when Bing came up to me

and said, "Look, mate, it's been great working with you I've had a right laugh… Look, you've got such a fantastic voice, why don't you get up there and sing!"

"I can't do that… not in front of Dickie Attenborough and everybody I'll look a right c**t!"

"No… come on," insisted Bing, "They'll love it!" Before I could stop him, he had leapt onto the stage and introduced me! Everyone looked at me expectantly, some of whom were saying, "Come on, Seebo!"

I thought, *Well, I can't bottle out.*

I climbed reluctantly onto the stage, looked at the sea of expectant faces and decided to launch into, "Start spreading the news… I'm leaving todaaaay!" when an extremely powerful jet of water hit me in the right earhole and swept me off the stage!

I looked to the right out of the open window and saw Paul Weston and Bing, who'd whipped outside, both hanging on to a fire hose and grinning like a pair of lunatics. 'Bing' had an air of total triumph as he paid me back for humiliating him in the piano bar! Well, that was it: the room started to clear as I wrestled a fire extinguisher off the wall and covered them both in foam.

The party descended into a massive 'food fight' with combatants who wanted to participate staying and those who didn't want to join in, like Dickie, Colonel Waddy and his wife, vanishing like magic to a far more civilised location.

The party ended with us all standing fully clothed in the showers, laughing like drains as we washed off all the tomato ketchup, mayonnaise, butter and brown sauce.

The next day they'd booked a unit outing, where they'd chartered a rusty old fishing trawler that we rashly took to sea on to catch some mackerel.

The 'top men' of the crew – Dave Tomblin, Steve Lanning, Bing and several others – were sitting on the bridge surrounded by crates of beer and having a game of poker.

We'd all been given packed lunches which consisted of a cold pork chop, Mars Bar and crisps.

We went through a shoal of fish and everyone was hauling them out of the water by the dozen… all except me. My fishing rod remained stubbornly rigid and never bent.

I became consumed with jealousy and started running up and down the boat to inspect what the other guys had caught, whilst berating the fact that I hadn't caught a thing.

Someone shouted, "Seebo… Seebo… look at your rod!" I looked and it was almost bent double!

Triumphantly I rushed across to reel in my catch, saying loudly to everyone, "Look at this! This has to be an absolute whopper! It's got to be a cod or something!"

I pulled it in and as I looked down I saw this grey shape approaching the surface, I hauled it out of the water to discover that it was one of our pork chops that someone had put on my hook for a laugh!

This caused a great deal of hilarity right across the boat and I turned to everyone and said, "YOU C**TS"

Paul Weston captured the whole thing on his super8 film camera and the denouement of his little movie apparently used to cause many laughs as the audience saw me silently mouthing the words, "YOU C**TS!"

I woke up the next day and already the rest of the APA had boarded the coach for the airport to take them home.

I rushed down to wave them off and the last thing I saw as it disappeared around the corner was David Auker leaning out of the window calling, "WHOAA MAHOMET, SEEBO! WHOAAA MAHOMMET."

I felt bereft; I was the last one there!

I wandered back in to the old folks' home to sling my gear into my holdall and set off on my journey to the seaport of Vlissingen to catch the car ferry to Harwich.

I was taking my little 2CV back to the UK.

I got in my car and started to drive through Deventer to find the road that headed South to Vlissingen.

As I drove through the town, I passed the two Paras who'd wisely decided not to participate in the crossing of the Waal.

I tooted my horn to them and they raised their arms in farewell.

I was twenty-two years old and I had the rest of my life in front of me so I decided to take my time getting back... after all, I had a pocket full of guilders and around £3,000 (£21,000 in today's money) waiting for me for when I got home.

I decided to take a detour through Arnhem and visit the war cemetery at Oosterbeek one last time to pay my respects and say goodbye.

It was a rainy September afternoon and for the first time in the six months I'd been out in Holland it felt a little chilly. I walked into the cemetery, which was completely deserted, and contemplated the last six months and wondered what was going to happen in the future. The rain had stopped and was dripping off the trees.

I definitely had the feeling that I was being watched, the more I wandered round the cemetery the stronger the feeling became until it peaked as, "Can you go away, please, you're disturbing us".

Slightly disturbed myself, I therefore decided to get back in my car and continue my journey homeward. I got to Vlissingen and boarded the ferry that set off at 10pm for the four-hour journey to Harwich, which passed uneventfully. By the time I'd cleared customs it was around 3.30am so I decided to park up and have a few hours' sleep in my sleeping bag, which I'd brought back with me.

I awoke in the back of my Citroen at about 6.30 in the morning and stared out of my window. Just waking after having bivouacked for the night were a small group of regular British

Paras getting their jeep prepared for the journey to Northern Holland to clear up the 1st Battalion headquarters.

I wistfully watched their red berets disappearing into the early morning mist… I would have given anything to be going back with them.

Anyway, onwards and upwards! I started the car and set off on my journey up the A12 back to my home in Suffolk.

Maybe Bob will give me my old job back on the farm, I thought as I drove through the Suffolk countryside I knew and loved.

I arrived back home and greeted my family; there seemed to be something not right and the atmosphere seemed a bit subdued. My father wasn't around, he was working on a TV shoot in Wales, and my mother was walking around distractedly with a

face like an extremely wet weekend.

I caught up with my brother Dan and spent the next few hours telling him all about what had happened on the shoot; he was alright for the first three hours but then his eyes started to cross and I thought he might slide off his chair! The poor devil's been listening to my stories about ABTF for the last forty years… I'm sure that's one of the reasons he emigrated to Australia.

Even now, if a member of my family has a problem getting to sleep, I just launch into a few *A Bridge Too Far* stories and it works every time… ten minutes later they're pushing up zeds!

I sat down to dinner that evening, after which Dan said, "Look, Seb, I need to have a quick chat."

He then proceeded to tell me that my father was having a serious relationship with a woman who owned the location on a TV show he was working on, in a sort of semi-hippy commune in Wales.

Oh no, I thought, *here we go.*

My mother tearfully confirmed the sorry tale.

So my parents were going to do what a lot of families started to do in the 1970s, which was split up.

My father came home a few times; I refereed the rows between them, and it was a relief when he left for good to set up home permanently on the hillside in Wales.

My mother was devastated and I felt so sorry for her. She was left with no career and no children, as my younger brother and sister found the idea of living on a commune in Wales with other kids and horses a far more appealing prospect than living with their grieving mum.

Mum and Dad were selling our lovely farmhouse and Mum was going to move into a two-up two-down in Colchester so there wouldn't have been much room for them anyway.

My brother Dan was also an actor and we decided that we definitely needed somewhere to live in London... but where? The vicars couldn't take us back at Hampstead. I bumped in to Farrell one day and explained our predicament to him. He said, "I've got two bedrooms in my flat, Sebaaastian, you and your brother can rent them, if you like."

Problem solved! So we moved in with Farrell in his three-bedroom flat in Brixton where we stayed for a couple of years. Good old Farrell, he definitely saved our bacon.

I then landed one of the leading roles in a new TV series called *Flambards*.

Maybe because of the exhausted state I was in and the worry about my parents' divorce, landing that job somehow didn't give me the joy it should have done.

And then it happened: our eyes locked across a crowded nightclub and I saw her.

That was it; I fell in love. I'd never felt that way about a girl before and we were planning to move in together and share our lives.

One evening I was waiting to meet her and she didn't arrive.

I telephoned her parents to see where she was.

"She's in intensive care," they said, "She was on her way to work this morning in the car and..."

For three days she hung between life and death and then she left us.

Life seemed to go a sort of 'white' colour with the word 'why?' 'why?' constantly going round my head I felt that I was viewing my existence through a white gauze on a film set where I could hardly hear or feel anything.

How her lovely parents were feeling at the loss of their beautiful only child I cannot bear to imagine.

The white gauze rose eventually to the scene in *Hamlet* where he says, "How weary, stale, flat and unprofitable seem to me all the uses of this world..."

I was never the same again, I gradually found my feet, discovered how to survive, but the joy had gone. Life in general no longer meant the same to me.

To all you young actors out there, don't think that being full of angst makes you a great actor.

To do your best work you need to be as healthy emotionally, physically and mentally as you possibly can be.

The years passed and like a damaged circus performer, I began to find the courage to step out again on the high wire of 'life'.

And then it happened again! I looked into the most beautiful pair of eyes again! Only this time, a year later we both looked into the beautiful blue eyes of our new-born son!

My wellspring of joy filled with a rush and despite taking deep draughts from it over the last few years has remained full to this day!

www.ingramcontent.com/pod-product-compliance
Ingram Content Group UK Ltd.
Pitfield, Milton Keynes, MK11 3LW, UK
UKHW021914190726
13853UKWH00002B/672